AMERICAN
CHAMPION

AMERICAN CHAMPION

AUTOBIOGRAPHY OF VIKTOR FROMMAGE

DUNCAN CULLMAN

LitPrime Solutions
21250 Hawthorne Blvd
Suite 500, Torrance, CA 90503
www.litprime.com
Phone: 1-800-981-9893

Published by LitPrime Solutions   11/09/2021

ISBN: 978-1-954886-51-3(sc)
ISBN: 978-1-954886-52-0 (e)

Library of Congress Control Number: 2021909465

Contents

American Champions (my teammates, gather
around me in our final huddle). 1

The Great Vacation with Daddy at ski camp
including the Master's great slalom 6

In Search Of The Lost City. 9

Sailing with Hans. 11

Dear Lions and Tigers 14

WAAAGH 16

African Savannah Bedtime Story. 18

Mary Monahan And The Flying Saucers. 21

Mary Magdalene of Morzine 25

2000 Years Ago Versus Today 31

Where went the cheerful days 33

Concession Speech. 36

Make America Kind Again 39

The Great Victory Speech (Thine Kingdom
Come On Earth As Well...). 41

Innocent! 44

Suree Suri has stolen the election (Walking
Encyclopedias Have Defeated Our Don) 46

Believe Because You Want A Happy Ending
(The Jewish Christmas Stories We Best Believe) . . 48

Christmas Story and Hanukkah. 49

Daughters of Jerusalem. 51

Dear Mia,. 55

Essential People and Essential Revolution 58

Homework Tonight and the lesson is to look
and see!. 60

God 67

My Father's House (The House of Israel). 69

Conquest of Mexico and Reconquest 1519-1521 . . 71

Mommy's Tart and Jam Factory 74

The Ascestion (Bill Ascending) La Asuncion
como Paraguay y todos de los países. 76

The Hunt for Mengele. 79

Heaven is a community 87

St. Littleton 89

Near to me 93

What are bears doing in Santiago?. 96

More of Jimmy On The Mountain. 99

Franny on Mount Everest. 104

"Young Pro Ski Racer" Hard Fast Life in the
Rockies. 109

My friend is a dog named Rusio. 115

BEARS VISIT SANTIAGO, a children's book . 118

Mrs Stone and the Mountain Shaped like a Volcano.................................121

The Monastic Life at St. Bernard's Monastery Ski Area........................125

My Brother Graham.........................129

Daddy's gone away 137

Arlene.....................................142

Tony Reynolds, the Monster, and my mother Thais, my Savior 144

Louis My Father............................147

The Secret Life of Louis Coleman............152

Eight Years Old and the Ark 157

Ana, La Santa..............................159

We Follow Jesus in our procesion 163

Gina,.....................................165

Trouble Near Times' Square.................167

The Monastic Life at St. Bernard's Monastery Ski Area...................................172

Flying....................................176

Skiing near Llaima Volcano in Chile with Rudel. 179

João Goulart..............................181

Boy at Ipanema...........................210

The Accident 212

Grateful 215

Gerry Knapp aka "The Knapper".............219

The Very Last Amateurs 224

James and John 228

Skiing in Peru part 2 234

Ronaldhino 235

Party Central Brasil 242

Pulque and Picaniyeu 245

When Liz came to shoot me 250

Pulque and Picaniyeu 254

Be A Soldier 259

We have a war to win 261

More of Jimmy On The Mountain 262

The warty hog (Warthog and tank destroyer) . . . 267

Pulque and Picaniyeu 273

When Liz came to shoot me 278

Perfect Pet 282

American Champions
(my teammates, gather around
me in our final huddle)

My lost and formerly wayward sons and daughters including those in between, I want to include you on my team because you have all played the game and been disappointed to have fallen behind through eight innings but now it is the ninth. It is yes the ninth inning and we are coming to bat. The opposing pitcher is tiring and his relievers are warming up in the bullpen.

I want you each to get on base. I want you to think about our team that we are here to win this great championship. Three solo home runs won't win this game for us. We need to load the bases then hit a double down the right field line. Then we need to move the runner to third base where a sacrifice fly ball will bring him home.

So when you step up to the plate think of me your captain. You voted me your captain because it is my last year with the team. I am older and will retire after this game. You will only have the memories of this moment in the years ahead when I am no no longer with you remember these our final moments together when we came together as a team to win.

You were all lost souls drifting in the streets but I brought you back to the sport you know so well to make you winners and give you my encouragement. Now we have become a band of brothers and a team of one.

The drugs you took did nothing at all for you nor the whiskey you drank to ease the pain was only delaying it. If you got "High" it was only temporary and followed by morbid depression and prolonged anxiety.

"To be on my team you will need to be sober" I told you and you finally believed me.

"I am your skipper. I am your captain. Now that I am old I finally brought you all together to teach you what I had learned so you will be wise. you will finally be wizards of the game."

"The opposing pitcher is not throwing strikes. He is throwing pitches that look like strikes but at the last moment they sink or curve or rise so you start your swings but must hold back and wait until the count is three balls because then he must deliver something honest, a true strike. Only then can you swing and deliver some power. It is not your own power it comes from grace and above.

Your God given talent comes only from heaven so it is not you who is the victor it is God who has entered you to win. God is a winner and the fallen angel is still falling. He is forever a loser.

This was all predetermined before we were born. It was predetermined that we should win this "World Series". It was predetermined that after losing an entire lifetime we would finally prevail and be the final winning team. We were born to have this great victory. It is the accomplishment of a lifetime of hard work, of fielding grounders and throwing to first base or to second and then to third and back to home plate. We took hours of batting practice.

My lost and wayward sons I have found you like a general on the battlefield and encouraged you to keep fighting and take it to the enemy's flank in a surprise attack from where he least expects it. Like a fifth column of soldiers that streams into the battle which appeared to have been lost but now will be won. I am your old and worn general. I am no school child any longer. I have lived many years and seen many continents.

My wayward sons and daughters you will be old like me someday and maybe you will be in my place as captains and generals with your own team with your own army to lead across this battlefield of life. There are those who have chosen darkness. They cannot win, they will never be competent leaders nor generals nor captains. Do not follow them; they have no discipline. They are lazy and drink until midnight and sleep until noon. The battle is over by nine o'clock in the morning. The troops rest and are weary but pick themselves up because they know tonight they will have to fight or perhaps by 3 AM.

Drink the water of life and yes drink water, plenty of it. This is the truth and listen to it. The deceiver wants to feed you conspiracy theories and bullshit to totally confuse you. The only conspiracy is that the devil is here in this world to deceive and kill you, to make a loser out of you.

So my sons and daughters which you are now since I

have adopted you because your own parents gave up on you, come to me and listen to my final words because a man who is dying can only tell you the truth and I am not dead yet but these are my latter years and I want to make saints of each and every one of you who is willing.

The existence is dividing between good and evil so you must choose a side to be on. If you want to win this final game and be a winner, then listen to me now. I realize that when I was young and lost like you were, I did not always give the best advice. As for the way I acted it was immature so I must apologize for my mistakes and errors, all those games we lost when the ball went between my legs or when I dropped the fly ball or made a bad throw. That is all behind us now. We are going to all be champions.

We rush into battle unafraid because we know the Lord is with us our shield and armor. We might suffer being wounded, we might die, it is true but God himself will lift us up to heaven because we are fighting for the right cause. We are not propping up some tyrant or demagogue by lying on his behalf for the sake of our enrichment.

There is a time for every season and a purpose under heaven wherein small jokers and fools must be replaced by men and women of courage who will step up to the plate. Do not be fooled by the enemy nor by the opposing pitcher who is throwing sinkers and spitballs.

I am here for you to lead you in this your cause of triumph over evil. I was born for this and so were you also born to be like your every idol because they were winners not losers.

Keep up the good fight. I know you will. I know you will step up to the plate this one last time. Do it for the rest of our team, do it for me because someday soon you will be just like me your captain. We shall all cross the finish line together. We shall all be winners in every sport and every battle. This is our destiny to listen to our peers take heed of their advice and encouragement and fight on and never give up/

I am like a quarterback and you are a receiver running into the end zone on the last play of the game, I throw the football for you to catch! Have hope, have faith and love the game and your teammates forever.

The Great Vacation with Daddy at ski camp including the Master's great slalom

O son of man who redeems the world with his sacrifice like a lamb

On the altar of this mother Earth where light is bent by gravity to form matter

Where are your disciples and when will they begin to listen to the truth

Only our love prevails and it was given to us a gift from God

Who so loved the world as to sacrifice his son upon a cross

Then he returned to us through our fondest memories those endearing moments

When we saw him love us like a best friend like God is to us and fills our every need

Keeping us humble in this suffering world we suffer his loss and distance

By distance squared everyone diminished four times in twice the distance

We are really not so far apart at all tis this illusion and these acts in time

To rectify our indebtedness every swear word and curse

We would rather have perfection instead we would rather be angels

But not yet as there are these chores and errands unfinished

Maybe God will complete them all for me with his love

He is my perfect friend in whom I trust my confidant I will tell him all

Then open my heart to others in his kingdom we are reborn all true friends

Of each other so please forgive me as we are mortal and temporal like the grass

We are green when young but wither in the drought and dog days of summer

Being us some rain and some mist from the sea to cool us with refreshment

I need your smile and cheerful eyes to restore my battery of love

Even my computer with its artificial intelligence knows the will of my father correcting every word perfect

It is the will of God that we did meet and I miss you so I have sent you my book

With the story of our lives so do remember me some dark winter's eve light your candle and read

To remember our fleeting days well spent in earnest to be friends forever

We will all be one together in the house of the Lord there are infinite rooms

One vast great vacation hotel where we will sing psalms and praises

For in the beginning before there was light there was music and yours still fills my ears with merriment and joy

When I was young and immature I thought I was supposed to win the slalom race and be great but now I realize I am supposed to win great friends and slalom around them

I love you all like a father at long last Amen

In Search Of The Lost City

In searching for the lost city that Citadel of our Lord in Zion

It is on the higher ground upon a hill not in a swamp

While I who am searching must confess I am lost

I am lost in this lower world now that I cannot see my Lord and Creator

I am lost in the darkness of night as though in a dense fog

When will the gentle mountain breezes return and reveal to me the sun and moon?

When will my star again shine and deliver the captives from bondage?

Then the Red Sea shall part and the highway be made clear for the escape of my people

We shall flee the oppressors and the Conquistadors and enter Vilcabamba

Refuge shall not be denied to us we will enter Zealand hut in the land of the living

Moses and Aaron shall ascend a high mountain and receive the Commandments of our God

Elijah shall prophesy that Jesus and John will baptize with water and fire

That the Holy Ghost will fill us with the love of our God

Wherein the land shall be made sweet with milk and honey Beulah

The redeemed shall dwell there and be fallen no more from the Garden

This is the second birth and the Resurrection it shall happen within me that I be new

Because I shall love the Lord my God therefore I shall love every man as my own brother and sister

So the Lost City I will enter and be lost no more for I am home with my God

Sailing with Hans

For some lucky reason we decided not to sail across Lake Champlain

Maybe it was all those white caps waves splashing

Maybe it was because there were no other sailboats in the lake with sails still flying

Two of them had pulled down their sails to troll with their motors

Hans's Lightning was too small for a motor and the jib was working just fine racing along the shore well still a few hundred yards out with Burlington still miles away

Maybe it was Susan screaming in my ear that he's trying to kill us I doubted that

Maybe it was the bow underwater like a German U-boat in the Atlantic

Finally at reappeared after a few nervous seconds waves pouring over us

Help bail some water Hans passed us a small bucket

Halfway across the lake or more the birds on Bird Island
had cried some insults at us proclaiming their niche

I screeched back at them all I don't want your eggs just
teach me to fly

Soon we were almost home to shore we pulled down
the sails as the wind still pushed us in it;s gail force

"Maybe we can sail next week?" cried Hans like one
of those birds I laughed in relief as it was almost over

Susan looked at me doubtfully but then she smiled when
her feet landed on the dock

Just another day on the lake beamed our Captain Hans

We haven't seen him in months as he's racing his dirt
bike over the jumps at age 67 pushing it a little as I
would say

It now is beginning to snow and ski areas will open with
Hans carving race turns like a madman

Well I suppose I am one of those too and Susan besides
me on her snowboard

She had even been a figure skater in her youth competing
in Stockholm when terrorists bombed the train station
beneath her window

I had my own thrilling moment racing my skis over
Tuckerman's Headwall

We were all much younger then but still our hearts
remain so

We fly like birds on that island in Lake Champlain
screeching our narrow niche in this world

We drove away as the red sun set upon our long day

(Each and every one of us has an incredible story as we
are all God's children)

Dear Lions and Tigers

All you very dear lions and tigers out there, is message is for you.

After you dine on all the rabbits and turkeys, chickens ducks and water buffalo there won't be anything left to eat and you will fight among yourselves until the last lion. That is why the Swahili bushmen are coming for you to protect the community" La Pueblita".

The tenth mountain division is coming down from the mountains and the ski hills to Washington. We are coming to protect the capitol from you radical extremists who love the lion and want to be lions themselves. The violence will end! You lions will be thrown in the cage to fight among your selves.

The people have spoken and the weasel has won the election. His followers are sheep, pigs and cows even geese, swans and deer. The "Pueblita" has risen up and will defend itself valiantly against you bully tyrants.

The "Pueblita" is protected by its covenant with the good shepherd, the Lord of hosts. The "Pueblita" is a loving community wherein all the species are protected, penguins and polar bears too> The "Pueblta" will defend itself against global warming and reckless corporations who endanger our environment.

I know you are lions and tigers, panthers and even

house cats, You can cease and desist in this senseless killing and re-enter the sheepfold of the "Pueblita" and be protected by the Lord or else face extinction.

The Swahili bushmen and the Tenth Mountain Division are on their way with the fire departments and the police to put out this bush fire.

"Law and order will be restored. Lay down your arms or face annihilation. The Lord has spoken. Let him who has ears listen. This is the end. Surrender or die"

WAAAGH

WAAAGH I am the president you voted me in because Daddy left me 431 million

Because I funded construction for fifty TRUMP TOWERS Waah

I am being cheated in this rigged election by DEMOCRATS

Backed by big interests and big corporations even my son says

We must GO TO WAR over these election results STAND BY KKK

WAAAGH

I've always had my way because Daddy and Geoffrey Epstein let me WAAH

I will be filing lawsuits to block any more voting which if against me MUST BE ILLEGAL

WAAAGH I hate to lose in fact for me losing is just not possible because I AM YOUR

The media has been very unfair in their socialist communist agenda for Marx and Bernie WAAGH

This election is being stolen by liberals and homosexuals with ties to CHINA

Where the virus was invented solely to defeat me and make AMERICA self-destruct into left wing Black Fatchism

Therefore I am calling out THE PROUD BOYS and THE KKK to fight in the streets

Until my eternal presidency is restored

I ALONE HAVE MADE AMERICA GREAT BECAUSE I AM GREAT Don't you dare forget it WAAAGH

"Donald, I want a divorce" Who said that? Waagh

WAAAGH!

WAAAGH KING Waaagh

African Savannah Bedtime Story

Once upon a time you heard this story already? The story about the mad lion who was also getting very old and maybe sick. He went on a rampage and began killing without eating, just killing for the sake of terrorizing the bush country,

In the village is the chief of the bushmen, an elder son of the former chief who was the son of another chief. He assembles the villagers to inform them that the old lion "has gone off his rocker" and "lost it entirely". So they need to sharpen their spears and go on a lion hunt.

This is necessary for the security of the little village "Puebllita" which has a different name in Swahili but means "Community". Thus the villagers grab their sharpened spears and head to the bush.

Meanwhile the few lions begin to fight among themselves as there are about two dozen of them in six different families or dens. The mad lion is killing all the game to starve off the other lions. There won't be any more food for the other lions so they know it will be better if someone kills him and now suddenly the bushmen with spears are running up the grasslands hiding behind trees in the savannah like "Savannah", Georgia where there aren't any lions except the one in Washington D.C. who has gone mad in the White

House but that's a different story, children? Maybe not so different, maybe there is a correlation with this story? Maybe the bushmen are the angels? Maybe their chief is God and the mad lion is our president?

"Oh no!"

"Oh yes, my dear children, the House of Representatives is meeting as we speak to impeach our president as he has gone off his rocker like this old mad lion!"

So this was supposed to be a bedtime story, but now it's becoming a nightmare of unprecedented proportions so let me go to the refrigerator with Mommy's permission to get some glasses of milk and cookies because we are all staying up all night watching MSNBC!"

Here come the bushmen. There goes the lion. They don't want to kill the wrong lion as the others are innocent of "mental illness". Our president went from mild sociopath to borderline psychopath with this pandemic now even much worse as he wanted his young lions to kidnap Nancy Pelosi and even Mike Pence maybe.

Turn the channel and watch the NFL and more combat there too so okay we'll watch the Hallmark Channel to escape reality completely. Why not take a break while the senate convenes and the bushmen sharpen their spears. We know this is not going to end well at all. Just ten more days in office for this sitting president who holds the nuclear football and might want to burn up the bush country completely? On the Hallmark Channel it is Christmas almost 365 days a year except for Easter when there will be an "Egg Hunt"

Now I want you children to know Mommy and Daddy love you very much even if the world out there is full of lions, tigers and alligators like Mitch McConnell. We don't know how to describe Nancy Pelosi as she seems off her rocker at times but maybe this president who wants to kidnap her has "pushed all her buttons to the extreme now".

I have decided like most Americans to get one hour of sleep as every channel is now a "Special Report" on some new atrocity this "mad lion "has committed.

Mostly there are unspeakable crimes, some involving underage girls in Moscow and some movies in which Vladimir Putin is the film director. Geoffrey Epstein is now in the movie too. Rudi and Eric are young lions? Rudi doesn't look that young. Maybe he has gone off his rocker too as he is a lawyer calling for "Combat".

I just want to sleep. I just want to sleep a long restful sleep and wake up refreshed with the bushmen carrying the dead lion on long sticks to the village to make lion stew. Too bad it had to end this way for this old lion in Savannah, Georgia where he has made a meal for everyone by his egotistical presence.

I just want to sleep again.

I just want to sleep but first I want you, my children to sleep. Yes, Mommy is tired too. She wants to sleep.

"Yawn"

We all have headaches and are taking Advil. It seems drugs are the American way and here to stay. Almost anything to sleep… this has been a nightmare for all of us in the community "Pueblita".

Mary Monahan And
The Flying Saucers

Almost like a stepmother to me was Mary Aldrich Monahan, a large woman in her latter years after the birth of her fifth child, Grace. She worked the Notch like most natives of the Littleton-Franconia-Lisbon, New Hampshire area. This was back in the fifties and sixties of the previous century now the 1960s. She had married another Twin Mountain native Leo Monahan who was the descendent of Irish Railroad workers who maintained the line through Crawford Notch by the Wiley House where an avalanche of debris had killed all the original settlers but spared their pet dog who stayed in the house.

Mary made famous milkshakes at Cannon Mountain Peabody Base in winter and made more famous milkshakes and sandwiches too at the Hugh Gallen welcome center a half mile north on the highway route 3 in summer which was passed by every motorist visiting the North Country back in those days as there was still no Interstate Highway like today.

Mary overworked 24/7 had developed diabetes along the way and her main fascination in life to escape her painful reality was "Flying Saucer Stories". Some colored man and his wife had reportedly been detained late on evening in the Notch while driving through looking up lo and behold it was a flying saucer on top of them. The man had been taken in and interrogated. The aliens spoke into a computer that translated their language into Eart Language like a modern Babbel decoder. The woman had been of less interest to the aliens and left in the car for the most part. Their story of course hit the tabloids within weeks and was thought by some to be nothing more than a publicity stunt. Mary Monahan thought otherwise and while Leo drove the car home every evening Mary kept her eyes to the sky to see if any space ships might still be lurking in Franconia Notch or nearby anywhere.

There was a junior in my high school class named Martin Cory whose parents owned the Cory Gunshop. Well Martin too claimed to have seen flying saucers and so understandably he was the victim of abuse by many of his contemporaries who viewed him as a bit odd.

Mary, on the other hand, read extensively on the subject and it was her understanding that the entire human race had probably been created not in any Garden of Eden but instead in a test tube as there space beings had decided to visit Earth and become inhabitants unsuccessfully due to its harsh climate including too much Nitrogen which somehow poisoned them with laughter which shortened their lifespans possibly though I would argue the exact opposite.

Thus the aliens found that they could combine their DNA successfully with Chimpanzees and so the bi-product of this was Adam and Eve and also the Old Testament. The original Jews were also space creatures or much closer to being so than other more modern races. This explains anti-Semitism as everyone is afraid of Einstein and his connection to God somehow he had a connection to the Alien Intelligence and came up with the Theory of Relativity plus the Atomic Bomb.

I began making my leather ski boots into fiberglass ski boots in the Monahan basement during this time with my boating fiberglass and epoxy kits and maybe the glue I was sniffing in this process was much too strong.

At any rate I arrived at Crystal Mountain Washington on a long expensive airplane flight to race Spider Sabich and the U.S. Ski Team who all marveled at my creations.

After losing the slalom by over five seconds each run I was greeted in the Finish Arena by laughing Spider Sabich who exclaimed,

"Take those boots off before you break your leg! Ha, ha, ha. I have to give you credit for not giving up. Good luck with that but I think you are barking up the wrong tree!"

After my inglorious defeat I flew back to New Hampshire and mopped the Peabody Base floors with Leo and his children while Mary fed us sandwiches and milk skakes she wasn't supposed to but why see her own children starve. Those were different days back then. At least I soon won the downhill at Madonna Mountain, Smugglers Notch with Earl Morse waving at the lower road to turn as i would have missed that entirely and broken into pieces. The Johnson State skiers knew how dangerous that mountain really was but I on my two brief runs failed to grasp the situation and skied the mountain like Jack Keroac let out of a looney bin with no restraints. I had no reason to fear anything on Earth as much as stories by Mary Monahan.

Mary Magdalene of Morzine

This world we live in is still not so perfect as Mary Magdalene ol Morzine in France.

I was briefly on the United States Ski Team, not so much as I deserved to be but more because Bob Beattie knew my father had money. Everything in America bought and sold though I was too young and naive at only nineteen years old to realize such a sad state of affairs.

While God in Heaven was trying to tell me something giving me these awful bone spurs on the heels of both my feet making skiing excruciatingly painful. This was caused mostly by frostbite from spending too many long hours in the cold. My feet froze often enough to develop hematomas which calcified every evening causing the precancerous boney bumps on my heels which made me punch holes in my ski boots rendering them less serviceable.

My ski coach Gordi Eaten from Middlebury not very sympathetic told me,

"Take another run! Keep on skiing until four o'clock, until the ski lifts close!"

He did this smiling at me on the top of Vail Mountain in Colorado with the sun setting and the temperature near zero Fahrenheit. His fellow coaches agreed as they were paying Vail for us to ski train there and now to get their money's worth, our many corporate sponsors like Lange Ski Boots and Bob Lange himself there offering to make me custom boots. Why had I refused? Was I nuts perhaps? At least the coaches agreed on that. Then on my 220 cm downhill skis running last in the rutted slalom race I had the third fastest time. Unbelievable but maybe Beattie was juggling the times as it was rumored he didn't like the midwestern athlete Jamie Paul because he was a late night bar hopper who preferred more fornication than hard workouts, a rich young man with most probably a very alcoholic father no doubt.

"The final and tenth skier and very last pick to go to Europe with the U.S. Ski Team is…"

All the young athletes held their breath and the room was dead still because each and everyone hoped to hear his own name but it was mine uttered instead.

We were being photographed boarding the plane for Europe and then landing in Marseille. We were photographed again though my teammates were puzzled still as to why they wouldn't let me off the plane in London. Was I some kind of a bad boy on the world stage somewhere or had my father done something?

The long ride in our suits and ties still up into the French Alps. We were going to Morzine, a very small town with a cable car crammed full of Frenchmen who didn't brush their teeth every morning. The downhill race course was demanding as it got you going eighty miles an hour then made some sharp turns. My precancerous condition zapped my strength and I kept missing some turns and in the race itself I missed them all but still crossed the finish line. The race officials were mad as hell. Was I some stupid American that did not follow the rules if you miss a gate pull over and stop. That required too much strength for me and gravity was obviously the true winner. My feet were sore indeed.

At the friendly quaint little hotel the owners were babbling in French. It seemed the servant girl or their daughter heard of my condition. I had missed one practice run talking in English with some French Anthropologists in the summit warming house. They were marveling at the shape of my head saying I was an example of indigrnous American Indian and maybe French as well as the Trappers in North America were first to breed with the native women etcetera.

The young lady about my own age insisted on bathing my frozen feet as though she was a healer of some kind and a fresh hot tub of water into which I put my feet was procured while I dressed only in a towel as instructed and sat back on my stool she washed my feet wonderfully. Gordi Eaton entered the room momentarily with a big smile on his face and said nothing then left as hurriedly as he had entered. I had a big scar on my torso from a childhood operation because my intestines had grown together and blocked the passage of my food. The young lady kept speaking French pointing at it then wept intermittently then prayed to heaven as though there was an angel there watching over us. She left the room still crying then returned with her parents plus Gordi Eaton plus Ken Phelps, my older teammate who served as translator.

The young woman was very infatuated with me and had decided I was the one she should marry. Gordi Eaton beamed again and said to me this only happens once in a lifetime. Would I please talk to her, get her address or just remain in Morzine indefinitely as a ski coach? He had never witnessed anything quite like this. Ken Phelps was talking to the parents trying to explain that I didn't speak French. They all seemed to agree it didn't matter. The young woman had seen" Jesus" while bathing my feet. She had a holy vision and Ken Phelps was telling me that that's what happens in Christianity when a woman finds her man she thinks he is Jesus. I admit I knew her game and being somewhat of an actor I had gone along with her imagination to make her fantasy come true. The young woman was totally overwhelmed. If I did not marry her immediately the parents would be insulted and we must leave the French village immediately.

"Marry her" demanded Ken Phelps.

"I can't even talk to her!" I protested.

It was very sad. I think I even began crying as we left because she was hysterical. Gordi Eaton in all his years ski coaching which soon became fifty remembers to this day our big altercation in Morzine. The young woman wailing. Her parents embarrassed and thought me to be a madman for leaving her. We were only nineteen she and I but in France that is the age at least back in 1967 it was. It was a long time ago and I am still not Jesus though moving in that direction slowly. Given the opportunity all over again I might have stayed there in Morzine and been a celebrity of sorts. We all think back on our livers and wonder about the paths we choose to go down. This one and not that one. Sad.

We left Morzine for Italy and Switzerland. Then Austria and home again.

Merry Christmas everyone and Mary too

I want to go back to France to love all its people. I want to find Mary

2000 Years Ago Versus Today

Over two thousand years ago a doctor named Jesus said that what can harm a man most is what comes out of his mouth even more than what goes into his mouth.

Now that we are all wearing cloth face coverings let us remember what our healer and doctor Jesus said because apparently he spoke the truth to some very high degree of proficiency. He was very knowledgeable more so than even our own president apparently.

Perdition and loss occurs to us when we speak falsehoods and make up lies about our neighbors even though it seems funny to us on the schoolbus when young to say that some other child's mother is a monster and/or that their house is full of field mice, toads and boa constrictors or perhaps they all practice witchcraft.

I am not Dr. Fauci nor a White House advisor on national health nor our president's personal physician and most of us don't want any of these difficult jobs such as president or first lady.

Apparently people though espousing to be "Christians" don't really adhere to very much of what Jesus the Christ actually said or did. We are witnessing an entire cult of self-proclaimed "Ministers of the Spirit" who have brought us to the brink of perdition and hell or else why are we experiencing these plagues reminiscent of "End Times of Our World".

"Go in peace, my brothers and profess the truth is what I have told you."

Therefore it is apparent that Jesus was our very best of friends and could be trusted as such even more than the majority of our so-called friends who lead us to the edges of cliffs and laughingly tell us,

"You can fly like Superman!"

Our president was wearing this outfit as a mild joke but maybe he was dead serious.

This brings us back to 2000 years ago when men were more advanced than we are today evidently. We have been backsliding into an abyss...

The blind shall see, the deaf shall hear and the lame shall walk in the Kingdom of Heaven in the presence of our Lord and Savior.

"I am the Way and the Truth and the Life, Nobody comes to the Father but through Me!"

"I am the Door, knock and it shall be opened"

Where went the cheerful days

Where went those cheerful days when I cheered for you silently

Or was that me yelling from the dugout as you rounded third base running for home plate?

And did we win every game I think not but we never cried about losing

Because there was always a game the very next day when I would hit a home run or wish to

You trapped the grounder in your mitt and tossed it to me on second base for the double play I threw to first (base)

Though good fielding never won a game we did that with our bats

Like Mickey Mantle and Yogi Berra we were a team and all our team mates can I remember some of their names just a few

We were smiling telling stories about that girl you dated she was a looker real fine

Whatever became of so and so and who ended up where

did they ever play ball again as the league folded after twenty seven years

Now there are no more games like that with all that yelling and camaraderie

Tennis is much more subdued me and my Mts. we took it up and we are better than most

It's just quite different a sport more to do with money and country clubs

Now we all wear masks in this pandemic at first they locked down all the fields and most of the tennis courts too

I hardly see my friends anymore though I talk with just a few on the telephone

We are waiting for the vaccine and a siren to sound the "All Clear!" but maybe it is just wishful thinking

As our friends in Peru do not write and this worries me I am afraid for everyone living in cities especially in poorer countries and especially the elderly that's who we are now

We are the elderly and our numbers diminish every year remember so and so yes he died

They found him in his car. He did drink a lot and it contributed…

Do not think about it too much remember instead our former days of glory when we all did shine like the sun

We were smiling because we won the big game you hit a walk-off home run over the center field fence he almost caught it but it bounced off his glove over the fence

Where went the cheerful days I still love those dearest of memories

I think of my best friends and hope this pandemic will end and we will all be out there again taking batting practice

We need to practice and play perfectly and depend upon each other with hope and trust and good will like perfect teammates...

Concession Speech

My fellow Americans,

Most of you did not even know I was running for president as my name did not appear on the ballot where you voted and even in grade school I had some difficulty spelling it correctly so you most likely would have also had you attempted to write me in.

One of my big problems was that I did not even vote for myself in this election though in years past I might have once.

It is difficult to lose especially considering that the other presidential candidates were of no special substance being both senile and argumentative with zero grace.

There is evidently not even one fit American for this highest office as we are all equally brainwashed by American television which contains commercial advertising telling us we must indeed buy everything in life including your vote. That Donald understood this particularly well when he tossed his MAKE AMERICA GREAT AGAIN hat into your willing hands and you were fool enough to wear it.

Now we have a nation of idiots like you who are wearing these baseball hats singing in unison,

"Take me out to the ballgame, take me out to the show!"

You think you are worthy to stand at the plate and swing a bat? The manager in the dugout is God. He will determine where you are in the lineup. You better behave well on the bench so you will even be included in the game.

If nominated I will not accept. If elected I will not serve. I am just a total loser which brings me to your vote of confidence in me and you never did cast it. Therefore I declare myself an American Indian very likely to return to my reservation you have prepared for me in the Mojave Desert. I best fill my canteen.

So I am on my way into the Mojave and Death Valley on that long road to nowhere totally unemployed as I lost my one chance for my very first job in life to be your personal President of these United States. Judging by the election results I would hardly think so.

You can join me there in Mojave please bring some blankets as I forgot mine and the nights are cold even lonely. Maybe we can find some stray dogs for friends if you bring a can of dog food. Once you feed them they never forget for a lifetime. Humans are not like that at all you may have taken notice that your best friends of long ago are nowhere to be seen. Exactly. Now we have the root of this problem; it is our human nature. No human is fit to govern over any other whatsoever. Only God has the right to judge us and decree our futures. You think you can do it by buying stock in my company you think you can own me like a slave? I thought we abolished that. Evidently not.

I concede that we were both slaves of that same system by watching American television. I was in Austria once where the TV was owned by the state and was just one channel so as not to confuse everyone like here in America where we watch "The Bachelorette". This is confusing as a grown woman has to kiss every potential boyfriend like some flippant teenager. no wonder she gets totally upset and cries. Each one wants to enslave her.

No one has given you the right to enslave another. Turn off that television please HD or 3D or whatever. Do not vote for me simply because I do not want the job of entertaining you daily on television which is now the job description of American President. We will be better off as a couple of unemployed in the Mojave because during the day there it is much too hot to work. At night our hands and feet might freeze. We might construct an adobe but without water we will not be there long enough.

I want to take this last opportunity to thank you for not voting for me as you would have expected something from me like an economy or a job to hire you. You are just standing there and not being creative inventing something. Why in the hell do you think I would want you on my team anyway? I'll pitch and you swing the bat if you can do anything at all, play ball

Make America Kind Again

Make America kind again and loving

Make her people thankful and full of grace

Make America love again because she is full of liberty

Her people are free and the devil has no place in our democracy

The people have spoken and those who rode the coat tails of the bully

Those whose faith was in the motormouth from Hollywood

They have ridden the magic flying carpet into a second Nuremburg

We will put them on trial and hold them accountable

There will be justice again because that is the fate of this world

It continues to rectify itself and proclaim the Lord like a hymn

Her people sing in the streets and cry for joy because salvation is near

In God we trust and He has delivered us that is why
we are great

We are great in truth and compassion and charity for
all in this the land of the living

Those who think Wall Street is great have leapt off a
high cliff

They have fallen into an abyss because they worshipped
gold

We still think it's great you can work and make a buck

But at the end of the day set up your very long dinner
table and feed all our hungry children

Feed all the world's hungry children because they are
crying out to be loved and cared for

Our international compassion and trust and belief in
human rights

This is what we love about America that America so
loves

Make America kind again and hear that ringing bell
of liberty across our land

We are a free people we are just and we do believe in
God we trust

The Great Victory Speech (Thine Kingdom Come On Earth As Well…)

My fellow Americans and also those who might want to visit our shores including those who never will to whom we send our warm embrace.

You might have heard by now that I lost my son and my first wife. What this means is I may be a lonely father without a family to receive my love so now you will be my family. I extend my love and gratitude to you all.

Now I have all this extra love to share (A father can save many children.). So now that I have won your votes I can be like a father to you if you chose to add me to your extended family. Add me to your living room on TV. Add me to your kitchen and boil some water for us so that we might have soup together where I may reside in your home at least spiritually if you so chose.

I want you to call me "Daddy". My house is a great white house but it is your house too. It is the house of all the American people who are winning this great victory we call love. Though there may not be room enough to fit all of you at once, feel welcome and think of this "White House" as your own. It belongs to the American people, not to some king. but to everyone who lost a grandfather because now I will be your grandfather.

And so my dear children all across America if America is to lead the world then I am speaking to everyone in every nation as well. It matters what a president says, yes it does.

Think of me as your great grandfather, a super Daddy who loves you all. I loved my own son so now I love you with that same love. I love you all because the health of this family, this family we call the world, the health of every family in this world is interconnected. If a plague or pandemic breaks out it affects us all. That is why we are endorsing a universal health care system to eradicate disease worldwide to prevent disease worldwide. Once these pandemics break out they are not so easy to contain and cost our economies dearly. They rob us of our extra vacation money but much worse of course they rob us of our loved ones.

They rob us of healthy workers in the fields to pick our vegetables and fruit. They rob the food right off our own tables to feed us. Once these pandemics attack they attack all of us.

So therefore my children,

Therefore you are my children everywhere. I have dedicated this speech to call you home. I am calling you to join me in one big extended family, the family of man where we will all be together. We are all on the same team now. There is no more "My team wins and your team loses".

We are on the same playing field: all of us are the winners here together who play the game. But "Family" is no game. Family is all of us together. That's whose president I must be to unite this nation, a president of each and every one of you worldwide who calls upon me.

If you can trust me then I can be your president.

This is both the victory and concession speech: that I love you all equally, of every race, creed color gender, of every political leaning. I will try my very best to be a good father to you all. This is how a president must serve his people. He serves the goodness of his own heart with compassion born from God to be shared among men as equals God is looking down from heaven ordaining a brand new day for our United States

Innocent!

If it may please your Honour, my client suffers from "Delusional Narcissism" in which he imagines he is being persecuted by Democrats who stole the last presidential election from him and his followers.

So in presenting my defense for him against the crimes he is accused of I entertain that he is a "Religious Leader" more than just a president. He has developed a "Cult" in which his followers believe they are destined to "Save America from evil Democrats and Communists" who persecute their divine righteousness.

You may therefore sentence him to prison like Adolf Hitler where he will write his memoirs and his "My Battle" for the sake of his persecuted followers the KKK, Proud Boys or other Christian Militia groups stockpiling weapons and filling twenty ton trucks with explosives to break him out in order to fulfill prophecy that "He is their true Messiah".

Therefore as a recompense for his crimes I suggest you sentence him instead to a "Psychiatric Ward" where he and his convicted followers with like offenses may all write volumes of directives for the "Future of America which will be great again".

These manuscripts can be published and psychoanalyzed by leading experts to reveal whether or not their authors suffer lobe epilepsy or miniature tumors of the brain causing such erratic behavior as to have become "Republicans" in the first place. It may seem they display abherent behavior bordering upon self-destruction and suicide in case their narcisstic demands are not met in full.

Therefore your Honour I enter the plea for my client of "Innocent by reason of insanity!"

Suree Suri has stolen the election (Walking Encyclopedias Have Defeated Our Don)

My Fellow Republicans.

There is a virus for one;and for two there is global warming. Drinking "Billy Beer" will not make these things go away. Living in denial of them has lost us this 2020 Pandemic Election.

There is one other key ingredient which relates to compulsive psychopathic lying. Should we follow a criminal cyber bully big shot just because he has a limousine plus a yacht plus a big jet and is a television celebrity we will do harm to the country even when our portfolios are enriched greatly.

So let us be smart rats all and jump off this sinking ship of this antichrist and false messiah who has no future. The devil with those who have misled us with cronyism from their bully pulpits of hypocrisy. Our true father is "Father Abraham" Lincoln for whom this Lincoln Memorial was built.

Donald Trump can be best remembered for the good things he did even though he seemed to have gotten lost in some dense fog or was it smoke from smoldering Democratic Institutions like Obamacare?

The American people regardless of ethnicity or gender identity now all have I-phones which they can use to boost their intelligence with simple questions like,

"Suree, who should I vote for in this election?"

So we must regard them as well informed even if they might have flunked life in general as at least they have these phones with 32 MG. These new phones can pass most written exams in a vast majority of universities.

Suree it seems has a doctorate in everything under the sun. Thus every Dick, Jane and Harry with an I-phone is now a walking encyclopedia. Very hard it is to lie to these people when you can hear in the backdrop someone named Suree has the answer and blurbs it out,

"Porkchops Pompeo and Pence are lying!"

"Donald assumes Melania won't divorce him in the next 24 hours but then when they are over, wait…"

"So please consider my candidacy, my name is Suree and my game is still the same…"

Believe Because You Want A Happy Ending (The Jewish Christmas Stories We Best Believe)

Assuming of course that God is Jewish and talked to Abraham then and therefore all the Jewish stories have happy endings like Job or Jesus rising from the dead to eternal life.

So therefore the stories with unhappy endings are not Jewish. He was a rocket scientist in Iran and the story has an unhappy ending. These stories are quite tragic and definitely more interesting. After all, heaven is quite boring but hell is quite exciting usually in a bad way with a bad ending.

Therefore if you are a writer you need to visit hell to have something exciting for people to read. Go to hell. There in hell dwell all the very profane demons, liars and murderers, adulterers and prostitutes. Sounds more like New York or Los Angeles or Berlin. Paris and Las Vegas you insist, okay!

This brings us back to the Jewish stories. Obviously nobody reads them in fact many are super allergic to them.

Once upon a time there was God. Oh, I lost you already? See what I mean?

Christmas Story and Hanukkah

God will save his people. He is coming again to save them and destroy their enemies.

Every story with a good ending is sent from God who is good and will deliver us so believe!

Believe like the little children because you want a happy ending.

In Sion Our Days And Nights Never Alone, copyright 2020 Duncan Cullman

6:20 AM

Our God is both with us and within us

Who is our salvation who restores us who gives us life

Who breathes our every breath who sees our every sight

He is not far distant on some other isolated planet He is on every planet

He is on every continent and with every person who calls to Him for help

If our president is godly then he is for us not against us he is a man of the people

Not above everyone not a superman but a common humble man

There are those who love arrogance because they are both ignorant and arrogant

Let them stumble and fall into the lion's pit let them dwell with serpents

Our God Who is with us His anointed will allow them their destruction

They bring it upon themselves who are without God and He is without them

God has gone on an extended vacation away from them who have no Holy Days no holidays

You imagine that God is in some distant place and He is distant from you

Come back to me my God that we may dwell together in Sion

Make Your sun rise and shine upon our day spent together and give us an evening together too with stars and moon

Daughters of Jerusalem

poem for Mia

O how lovely are these my daughters in Jerusalem

How will I find soldiers of virtue for them to marry?

Where is my army of righteousness to defend the government of Sion?

Young maidens become lost and think emeralds of topaz can save them

Turquoise cannot even save itself it lies in pawn shops abandoned as a false prophet

My daughter it is your own father who will escort you down the aisle into the arms of the man you shall marry on your most happy day

It is still rumored that a woman cannot see Jesus only her spouse

He becomes like Jesus unto her, a savior and father to her child who will be her messiah

She divorces the antichrist and wanders in a wilderness eating mana and honey

Where now is her daddy to save her from perdition and false accusations of the high priests

Who call her a harlot or a wicam or a cougar

Is her daddy still living in a far province perhaps in Canaan send word to him

His daughter now wanders this earth as though lost in a desolation full of jackals

Escape my daughter escape from the ungodly and unrighteous

Because your father still loves you like his father and the father before him they hold you in high esteem

As does God their Father who wishes for your return into the sheepfold

Like a Pastor is our Lord God full of righteousness and love for all his children

Especially for those who become frightened in the storm whose boats have broken masts

There is a tall pine to lay down its life that your ship sets sail on a new course

You have always thought about America and or Africa so set sail again

Set sail and remember Daddy is with you like your Grandaddy and Great Grandaddies God can be with you

Your new man you have found him and he will steady your course upon this rough sea

This rough sea of global warming and Charleton Despots with their misled understudies

The lost always follow the lost while you have found new direction and hope

There is still hope for you in Sion that you shall reside there in peace and tranquility

So take your father's arm because he leads you into the aisle en route to your beloved

You were a child playing with dolls and emeralds but now you will be a grown woman and see

You will see through the eyes of your beloved because he has binoculars to show you a new land on the horizon

You will travel there and have children, cats dogs chickens rabbits goats geese

Your new family awaits your arrival you were a princess but in Sion you will be her queen

So I'm not looking for someone to walk me down an aisle to meet God.

I'm not a harlot, lesbian nor cougar... I'm a person.

What I am is a 41 year old woman who never wants to ever get married again and have a guy tell her how to live her god damn life least of all a relative I don't know very well.

Just needed to clarify this...

Not looking to be saved. I save my own ass everyday...

Don't need any male figures... miss my Grandfather that is all.

Dear Mia,

This is just poetry not aimed at anyone. We perceive you are individualistic and? or Lewis wanted to keep you under the umbrella of his love and the trust.

Your job at vail stifled your artistic nature the other lobe of our brain where I write my poems evidently.

So be glad there is a queen in Zion Zion as the Talmud is very anti-feministic male rabbi dominated society

We certainly hope you and your dogs are ok even if you disown us or the umbrella of our love for you

You are still of the hormonal age and in a few short years you won't be so much that way so easily upset by others I don't know what you went through at Vail but Pete Seibert owned it and verbally attacked me when I drove in to park for a pro ski race 1971 I think it's prob a racist society there and Bob Beattie was himself quite appealing to white people mostly. A negro came to join the IPSRA basicly world peo and Beattie got rid of him in a few weeks but he filmed me and thought perhaps I was the first negro in the sport maybe we are a twinge but your ancestry DNA didnt indicate it, the native seminoles of Florida and Alabama were very dark skinned

Perhaps you are a Medicine woman of the Navajo we certainly respect you and encourage you to do your thing go your own direction whether you ever visit us or not

I haven't seen you very often your mother put a restraining order on me and she filed the divorce at that time I did not leave her as she claims

I had a lot of problems with my fathers associate or secret associate that Nazi pilot Hans Rudel who had in Germany a 1/8 jewish wife he left behind in East Germany, Hahn and we think she had at least one son or two

That former us women's coach and president of Marker bindings speaks fluent German and told me Rudel was "his father" you prob met that guy hank henry whatever

I have no definite proof Lewis was a cia or a secret service or a yale skull and bones just circumstantial evidence he never admirred anything

but in Darien he told me "Lipsky was a great man" a polish jew who was ambassador to Berlin and became Herman Goerring the nazi's friend

Lewis had some deals going on "BUSINESS" like they say

We love you and consider you and your dogs ALL MEDICINE PEOPLE so keep doing your dance, DAD and Sue

Dear everyone you are all dear to God or he she would not have created you for your special purpose,

We are having an allegorical discussion of Jewish law and I have no law degree so my only understanding of it is through reading the Bible or Real Estate Law as pertaining to Real Estate contracts.

I dare say that probably Trust Law is derived from the same place and has its origins in the ten commandments

Because we who were born outside Jerusalem are wild indians unlike Grandpa Lewis

We all loved our grandparents much more than our parents'

Now onto business hmm well Nikken and Jim are in charge and interpreting the last will and testament of Lewis and Josep B9 Benjamin means WOLF) Cullman. The Cullmans had no rabbis that I am aware of other than John Hall, the Bishop of Camridge who's granddaughter married Lewis grandpa or great grandpa in London. The Wolf's Lewis mother had Sephardic after Sephardic rabbi ancestors who crossed Africa living mostly in Morocco Spanish Morocco and then at the Expulsion by Ferdinand of all non Christian THE INQUISITION whoever was in Spain and asked to leave some went to Canary Islands Azotes in router to America and some went to Holland as it was controlled by Spain at that time Dutch Deutsche not much different.

In any case we miss you and wish you a very Merry Christmas which has something to do with Jesus and the Bible, if you are a very liberal then all of that came from maybe space and flying saucers whose pictures are on cavemen walls somewhere. Dad and Sue

Essential People and
Essential Revolution

If God has created us we are all essential our entire lives

We work to sustain ourselves and no matter what we do

It is essential that God must think it so thus no one is nonessential

As for non-essential business there are those who break our laws

Our laws and commandments were decreed for our own protection

The transgressors once caught and sentenced go to our essential prisons (to be essential prisoners)

Now Christ is coming to free us all from sin and death and open the prisons

To redeclare that our work here on Earth had been essential to His return

We are all His essential people especially when we pray to be so

You regimes in power that consider us and our businesses non-essential

You are playing God but you are not God you are blashemizing your non-essential doctrines

Awaken all you essential lawyers stop cowering before the bench

You were born to defend the people and the laws and the Constitution

Or if not then there will essentially be an essential revolution

Homework Tonight and the lesson is to look and see!

For everything be most glad

Because God is constantly at work

Bringing us to His Salvation

Through every little thing is our grace to be perfected

Everything is by His Gratitude toward us whereby we might see Him

As He actually is because we actually will behold His magnificence

From the New Jerusalem which is perfect as is a diamond

There in the Garden of Eden guarded by the cherubim

Now we see in a blurred vision but soon we will behold what we sincerely believe to be true

Is indeed true that we are not alone and never were.

Our Creator has created us in His very image

For if not how might we imagine Him? He is no alien:

It is Satan that he alienated us from our true compassionate selves

To form us into an image of selfishness and greed, lust and debauchery.

Rise up from death now mortal man for your Day shall come with no sunset

When your doubt and despair shall be overcome

Then you will need your earthly body no more but shall obtain a new heavenly body

You shall be mine alone in paradise and forevermore.

So be enthusiastic about this final truth which will prevail

We will all be together again with seraphim and cherubim

Where night cannot go because the illumination of our God

Is everlasting and permeates all existence

So have faith that what I say is true, that God cares

And shall deliver us to this great victory to be with Him

Where He shall wipe away every tear and replace all sadness and doubt

With hope and a great enthusiasm called praise and thankfulness.

We who are unappreciative cannot endure any hardship and so we wither like the grass

Because there is no sustenance in us if we do not believe

This is our lesson and homework here because we are students

Most eager to understand the very meaning of our earthly lessons.

So I grab my pen and make some notes that I might remember

Lest I ever forget my enthusiasm for the truth that I might behold

From this blurred and obscure existence here in a world of misunderstanding and confusion,

Everyone is fighting and afraid which is most exhausting,

So we require sleep and dream of what went so horribly wrong

Yet this brings us back to our lessons learned.

So the very next day we rise up refreshed of good conscience

Or not rise at all and sink into despair and death if hope is lost.

We hope our teacher RABBI is present here among us

For without our shepherd we are lost sheep and leave the fold

To face utter destruction and run off some cliff chased by a bear.

I invite you to study and learn, open up a good book and read

What God has spoken is all your homework tonight

If it is home that you long for then come

Or else be lost at sea where the great serpent shall devour your ship.

Do not let yourself be sunk but see the great lighthouse

Which beckons you home to those that love you

God is Alive!

3:03 AM

Write all these things down when the people are ready to receive new knowledge. Write down that once forgiven they will not suffer the past because now is their new day of liberation and love. They will be free.

Love is coming to save them because the Master is perfection and living in divine perfection. In the fullness of love there is no past and karma(debt) is released. So are the children of Israel released from bondage and slavery in Egypt and given the promised land which is this brand new day of now. As for tomorrow do not worry about it because with the past now forgiven the dharma duty of tomorrow is light. The burden and yoke of past sin is released and the beast is no longer like the oxen needing to be whipped. These new oxen gladly work because they are loved so they know all duty is just to love and be loved.

As for tomorrow, have faith that Our Father shall take care of us like the birds, do they reap and sow?

Write this all down because the people are ready to be united in love in a united state of love. Young people suffer because they are overwhelmed by their senses of touch, smell and taste.

There is an evildoer in this world whose past is notorious and for this reason he does have the very most dismal future possible. He will be put in chains and thrown into a pit for over one thousand years in a lake of fire where there is no water to drink and his own throat will grow parch like a man lost on a hot day in the Sahara.

Now you my children will not go with him nor be lost because love has found you. You are now so loved by God your creator who speaks into your hearts with the utmost pleasure which is love itself.

Those who love will establish the kingdom of God which is what every family desires, a perfect home, where all within are loved and cared for and each cares for the other. They dwell like sheep in a flock because the Great Shepherd is there with them standing guard. If one gets lost the shepherd retrieves it and brings it back into the herd.

This world will not endure forever but the kingdom of God is eternal and shall always. There has been just too much sin here on Earth and its secure present is unsustainable. It's very karma of debt to sin is gloom and doom. When you watch the nightly news you realize that evil has had its own day but those who follow wickedness are being chased by the police. It shall always be that way. The devil is on the run being pursued and will find no sanctuary.

In the meanwhile you shall be saved because the Master Himself talks to you and tells you this is how it will be as you grow older and wiser. God himself will try to find a way into your heart if you are willing to listen and be loved. Then you shall hear the Word of God which is Love and you will love others as you wish to be loved yourself because God loved you when He She created you.

I am sorry we must all die one day for our sins because of our ignorant ways this is our dharma duty to return to God and dwell there with God in His Holy City New Jerusalem. On planet Earth the old Jerusalem is still at war and being besieged by the nonbelievers.

They were unable to kill the Master because He did not sin and thus returned where his disciples beheld his full Glory. We shall all soon reign with Him in Paradise and in the meanwhile we invite His Kingdom to be here on Earth in our very presence. We go to church and pray if we are too weak to do that at home or under a tree in our garden.

So pray to your living God because there is no other. Balzebub has no future and his followers end up in despair, panic and bad conscience like psychopaths. Do not follow him like a sociopath. There is no future in lawlessness but prison where all are tortured at least mentally if not physically abused as well.

Come to New Jerusalem I beseech you in the name of my Father. There is no other place of refuge but with God himself herself. She he is waiting with open arms for your return, now come my child and be with the Master your Pastor and take your place in peace and salvation

God

Our God we have made a covenant with loves us conditionally. If we love our God then we are treated favorably, so we pray.

We pray that any references to God as a woman will be forgiven. She is most lovely under the apple tree, the daughter of Jerusalem and her banquet is love.

God himself is not exactly love but requires obedience? Jesus loved us all unconditionally like a father not conditionally like a mother who may have spanked us.

So New Jerusalem is where we will live and she is a diadem like a diamond in the sky. She is lovely as the angels are who protect her. Jerusalem on the Earth is the geometrical center of the land masses or nearly so. She is hidden by a cloud of moisture wherein her flock of sheep and the children live protected by God. They also must choose to protect themselves however God instructs them.

An atheist is still loved by God as are the heathen who wander like vagabonds who flee lands of lawlessness knowing that somewhere there is justice in the land of the living.

If I lie to you then this is terrible karma and my future is surely in doubt because the dishonest will not see God. They are liars and sorcerers, everything vile and offensive.

Know the truth and preach the Gospel of Jesus Christ because he is faultless and pure. He never lies to us even though his parables sometimes bewilder us.

If God loves us conditionally because of our covenant then some people might be confused and think God is our mother. There is some confusion because Baal the fertility god of the heathen was like a golden cow.

Surely most of us in this modern educated world of I-phones are not like the Incas in Vilcabamba worshipping a large rock from the Ice Age deposited at the edge of the Amazon.

Hyana-Capac, the last Inca, said before his execution in Cuzco, Peru

"Look my people how I am being executed by these invaders with their own God whose son is Jesus Christ"

God please forgive me if I have erred or told any falsehoods and or lies. Miryam from Argentina wrote me to tell me that the Hebrew God is never a woman. Therefore I must clarify myself in the eyes of God.

There are some other thoughts I have been given but tonight I am not to write them down so these clarifications are back in their cloud which is the mind of our Father from whom all our truths originate

My Father's House
(The House of Israel)

Take sanctuary and rest in the House of the Lord of Israel

It is your father's house and was his father's and was Abraham's

It is a rock and a church this House of Israel to save you from the storm

You cannot purchase it because God who dwells within and without is also not for sale

Do not insult God and think He may be owned so do not attempt to buy His house

There is of course the house of perdition, the synagogue of Satan do not fall into that trap or snare

Live instead one hundred years in peace and understanding

The king is coming the king of Israel and the house belongs not to him but to his heavenly Father

So dwell instead in a yurt or a tent or pay rent or be a house sitter to be safe

It is the Lord Himself Who owns this house of sanctuary in Zion

Go instead like Ruth and purchase a field to plant some seeds that there will be a harvest by the righteous

Because not all who sow will reap and so not all who dwell in houses will be happy

Only those who take refuge in the House of Israel shall escape this current storm

This raging fire and this raging virus, these tornados, hurricanes and earthquakes will consume

Everyone who dwells in the houses of perdition shall become lost in the sea of fire

Therefore take rest and sanctuary in your Father's house because you are a child of the Lord who is his Lord

Try to understand this, fathom wisdom and be a sage very learned

That you may live in peace forever with God

Conquest of Mexico and Reconquest 1519-1521

There was a man born in Spain, Hernan Cortes in 1492, who was a Salvador (Savior). He was granted then rescinded an expedition to map and then to colonie New Spain (Mexico), the inhabitants of which offered sacrifices to their two faced deity Huichilobos and Quetzalapan. The hearts of those sacrificed were pulled from their bodies still beating. The walls of their temples covered in blood and their priest's hair matted in dried blood as those same priests mostly dined on human flesh, One hundred thousand human skulls were on display with two hundred thousand human thigh bones.

I have heard it said that Christianity is practiced by hypocrites who preach love but wield a sword of destruction and death. Hernan Cortes was much above all that as he told the natives that they, the Spanish, wished to be their brothers and would they refrain from human sacrifice as the Christian God forbids it. The natives were indeed very restless and slow to convert though the chiefs(caciques) of many provinces soon allied with the Spanish as they had been robbed and brutalized by the centralist Mexican government whose leader, Montezuma, confiscated their sons and daughters for human sacrifice plus demanded tribute in corn, chickens fish cotton jewels gold and silver.

There is a parallel here with Hannibal who invaded Italy, the provinces of which paid burdensome tributes to Rome until Hannibal liberated them and conscripted them in rebellion. Cortes was very smart in every instance unlike Pizzarro who was one of his soldiers who later subdued the Incas.

Hannibal was the most brilliant general who ever lived but was driven from his lands of conquest to be defeated in his home country, Carthage. Cortes was driven out of Mexico;s city fort in that lake just once but retook it with reinforcements sent to arrest him whom he also captured and convinced to join his command. He is like George Washington, a great leader of men and most probably more eloquent.

It is said that the Spanish and Ehineland Germans (Swabians more specifically) were once one tribe living near Paris that split apart so they are distant cousins. In this regard Cortes was like those German Gauleiters of each province who commanded and educated at least their officers and sometimes their entire army with great oratory and pomp giving inflammatory speeches convincing their troops before any struggle that destiny was on their side that even if the battle was long and costly they would win and the fight was that which they were born for to achieve glory.

I am so lucky to have found this original story in its 492 pages and promise myself to read again another large text of the defeat of the Incas to reassess Francisco Pizarro.

I was once on a stopover in Mexico City for a two day layover on my way to Chile. I walked through parts of it with no idea there had been so many battles fought where I stood as in my high school we read all of Mexican History in two pages and thought like most teenagers we now knew everything about Mexico and Mexicans or the rest would be revealed on television, quite the contrary. We learn only what our leaders want us to learn so for the most part we are held in ignorance. Our minds need to be conquered like the mind of Montezuma whose priest of Huichilobos had prophesied of conquerors who would come from the rising sun to overlord them all and expand their minds that there was indeed a new higher moral code more ethical in which men might all be like brothers to one another and not just ne slaves and cannibalistic masters

It took 93 days the Battle of the Reconquest with a three pronged attack into the Lake City of Mexico during which all the beautiful houses and gardens separated by innumerous canals were flattened and the debris used to fill the canals in utter destruction to insure it would never be rebuilt nor any future indigenous revolt be successful. One of the most beautiful cities in the world was flattened in order for its people to realize that Christianity had indeed conquered them while their last Prince Cotopac and his family were left alive the remaining 12,000 were slaughtered rather than surrender. It had been a city of over 300,000 people, the survivors of which lived in its suburbs had wisely embraced alliance with the Spanish invaders who had muskets, long swords and muskets.

Mommy's Tart and Jam Factory

When Mommy came to town

She brought jams, jellies and tarts

Wasn't long before Daddy took notice

Down to business, nose to the grindstone Mommy

She wanted to make her mark in the world

Then take it to the bank and cash

Procure good credit and live in a very big house

Next to the Post Office, shipping and receiving

She would receive dedication and devotion

While spreading her contagious love

For all creatures big and small

While breaking for small animals on the highway, even insects

Reptiles included, Armadillos and Guinea Pigs, Marmots and Porcupines

Birds build nests in her window where the storm window was missing

They hatched their young which flew into the driveway

To watch Daddy barbecuing some Kielbasa and Bratwursts

She brought her eleven year old cat with her which Daddy;s dogs soon respected

Even admired when home alone the Kitty took charge of those dogs like a pet sitter

Mommy was down at Farmers Market downtown

She had a heatstroke complicated by Covid 19 Pandemic

Now she is back in heaven with the angels still busy as a bee

Definitely not enough jams and jellies in this world short of sweet tarts

Writing all these verses I've grown hungry and decided to make toast with butter

There are thousands of jars of jam and jelly, no shortage whatsoever

She's up there with God at shipping and receiving

Still spreading her love to all creatures great and small.

The Ascestion (Bill Ascending)
La Asuncion como Paraguay
y todos de los países

48 hours have passed. It is the third day and my Rottweiler is consoling me over the death of my rival friend Bill McCollom who was one year my senior at Holderness where we really didn't like each other very much. No one expected him to die so suddenly.

I sent him my poetry book and maybe that didn't help him at all. We were such rivals over fifty nine years though for some of those we were doing different leagues of competition. He went ski jumping and I went professional slalom. Neither one of us made the Olympics though our dreams were indeed that big. He managed to complete his education at Middlebury College where I had originally wanted to go but they never gave me the time of day there nor Dartmouth as back in those days they were 95% white.

I don't need to overthink this story much. His best friend at Holderness Terry Morse of Aspen almost died skiing into a tree at Jay Peak, Vermont where it was twenty below zero and my father saw the accident from inside his very large fur coat that wouldn't even keep him warm. A tree branch went through Terry's jaw and the cut the branch with a chainsaw taking both the branch plus Terry to the hospital. He lived. Bill and Terry were avid ski jumpers. I didn't excel at Nordic skiing but was expelled from Holderness for flunking English. I taught my Pakistani roommate David Nichols to fight and he attacked my bully English teacher Fleck. I suppose I got the blame for that too.

My Rottweiler looked out the window at the clouds. Bill McCollom is risen and gone to heaven where the music of the angels and their language is of such beauty anyone hearing it would never want to leave there in the first place.

We have all been sent to this Earth by our Heavenly Father to learn perfection and grace. Bill learned it with a 4.0 average. He mastered the lesson here and so has risen. Most of us so they say will not make it where he has now gone. It is very brilliant there near the Lamb who sits upon that Throne at the Footstool to God whose radiance and Truth is blinding for He is all knowing and has every eye seeing everything and knowing everything and now he congratulates Bill McCollom who has a new name like "Saint" and the Lord is very pleased with our friend who once was Bill but now has risen. Meanwhile back on Earth, a very dismal place by comparison, eighty eight volunteer utility outfielders need be found to take Bill's place on the Mound and in the dugout as Manager as well.

The Waterboy has been given a glove and was just told to play Right Field.

Of course meanwhile back in Heaven they are playing "Ode to Joy" and Handel's "Messiah" as well as

Mozart simultaneously and all this music miraculously blends together to make a sound far to sweet for human ears. It seems God needed a new Manager for Heaven so he recalled "Bill" from the Earth that very morbid place of untold human suffering.

The Hunt for Mengele

Josef Mengele was born into a family which manufactured trailers that were pulled behind trucks and cars and horses. The family had been in the business probably since the days of Otto Von Bismark who had united Germany in 1871.

He was an avid alpinist, skier and ice climber Josef Mengele born around 1905 in Westphalia near the Rhine River near the French and Luxembourg borders. Josef enlisted in the ski troops mountain division as he was thirty four years old when Germany invaded Poland. The draft was compulsory in the New Nazi Germany of Adolf Hitler who proclaimed himself "Fuhrer" or leader. That was that as democracy was blamed on mosat of the world's ills and this was now replaced from necesity of the German people, an Aryan race, destined to rule the planet soon after the 1936 Olympics in Berlin where Germany won the most medals everything but not the track event won by an American negro Jesse Owens.

Mengele's division was quickly attached to the German Fifth Panzer Division assigned to break out the entrapped Wehrmacht Army of General Joachim Von Paulus surrounded by the Russian Army at Stalingrad lead in the end by General Nikita Kruschev who would one day be the Premier of the U.S.S.R. as well as Communist Party boss.

It was a very cold winter that one in Russia 1941-1942 and the tanks of 5th Panzer division attacked northward in snow and ice but ran out of the precious ingredients for their engines ethanol which the Germans were first to produce as their petroleum supplies were running very low after General Rommel's defeat in Afrika. Fifth Panzer division came to a grinding halt and then and there unable to move when the Red Army discovered its position and lobbed every imaginable projectile destroying most of the 5th Panzer Divisions heavy tanks.

Josef Mengele jumped onto the turret of one burning Panzer and pulled more than two komeradden to safety and became a war hero transported back to field hospitals and then to his hometown to recuperate from his burns. His wife later declared that Josef's ambition had overcome his reason when his old professor telegraphed him to ask for his assistance at Auschwitz Internment and re-education facility in Poland. He acquiesced and departed thereafter in 1944 to play a leading role in "The Final Solution" which Hitler and Heinrich Himmler, a chicken farmer, had drafted for the extermination of every Jew in Europe. Often Hitler's motorcade stopped by a small picturesque lake near Rosenheim where the Fuhrer enjoyed a picnic on his rides between Munich and his residence at the Eagle's Nest which had a view of often snowy mountains. The Fuhrer detested the winter and its snow preferring more summers with frivolous Eva Braun and their dogs, Blondie the German Shepherd being one.

Mengele became quite engrossed injecting gasoline into twins of the Jewish race that he had saved for his experiments. Sometimes he injected substances into their eyeballs to change their colors. He even had a collection of these various eyeballs of different colors on his office wall after they were removed and soaked in formaldehyde most likely. He also saved an eight year old White Russian looking Jewish girl possibly named Nona Okun. He sterolyzed her and kept her in his office as a pet or companion for his loneliness as his wife remained at home in Westphalia sending him letters bearing the family news.

"Dear Josef, You must remember the kindly neighbors whose sons were sent to the Russian front in Operation Barbarossa to give us all "Breathing Room"(Hitler called it) Well the news is bad as they haven't returned but they did at least die for the glory of the Fatherland (Germany) to defeat those barbaric Bolsheviks."

The girlfriend of Mengele was shipped to another camp and possibly one that was quickly liberated by Russian troops so she quite possibly had survived. This brings me to Nona Okun who looked tall and skinny like a White Russian but she was from a kibbutz in Israel arriving at Portillo, Chile proclaiming herself to be an alpine ski racer from New York State (which she had visited briefly).

At any rate maybe as a child in Russia she had cross country skied in gymnasium class or the like in USSR before escaping to Israel. I was sixteen years old when I met her and she confided to me,

"I was in Argentina in a small town and suddenly there in the same town Mengele came walking across the sidewalk after buying a newspaper. I was astonished to see him still alive and in better health than me. I wonder how he escaped capture?"

As a ten year old child I had read William Shirer's "Rise and Fall of the Third Reich" all 1,100 pages describing atrosities committed by Nazi doctors in the name of medicine, freezing couples in bathtubs etc etc. Nona wanted me to be friendly to the tall blond German man on one ski with his one leg and arm stabilizers with little skis attached. She told me to go up the ski lift with him as he would without doubt invite me to visit Bariloche, Argentina which had now become a Nazi hideout where Dr. Mengele was sure to show up as he was attached to this one legged German, Hans Ullrich Rudel (Stuka pilot).

Rudel explained on the ski lift that I would please ask the Chilean Ski Team chaperone Mrs Leatherby-Gazitua if I could travel across the frontier from Chile to Argentina with them as I was a minor which meant that without an adult accompanying me I would be unable to cross borders. Just three months prior in Alpine Meadows, California I had ridden up the ski lift there with this very same man but maybe I thought this was his twin brother or something four thousand miles south or did he fly everywhere like a bird?

My own father would someday ask me why I had decided to conspire with these foreign terrorists,

"Just exactly what was in it for you?" He drilled me at the dinner table out of the clear blue sky ten years later when I went to visit him in Connecticut years after his involvement with the CIA.

The plan which was formulated by Rudel and Mrs. Leatherby was that I was to take the narrow gauge train, the only train in Chile, from the South Metropolitan Station to Osorno where I was to meet up with my Chileans ski Team friends including Veronica Saez who would one day marry a Chilean Army General, and Ricardo "Dickie" Leatherby and his chaperone mother who would later save my life.

After sharing my banana with Mapuche children in the South Station I boarded the train and to my surprise the one legged man came walking by finding me. I felt uncomfortable but then he invited me to the front of the train where I shoveled some coal into the engine. It was a steam locomotive. Then the conductors and Rudel told me to go back to my seat.

In Osorno I departed and told the taxi driver the name of the hotel Mrs Leatherby was to pick me up next morning. The Chilean ski team had gone ahead of us but Mrs Leatherby had decided to spend a night or two at the various hotels at each end of the Lake of all the saints, "Lago de Todos los Santos" east of the Volcano Osorno but west of Cerro Tronador also a volcano but thought to be dormant now. In those olden days in the Andes there were no plowed roads and crossing the Southern Andes was only possible by a sled caboose pulled on a chain by a bulldozer between several lakes below the snowline usually.

There was now no sign of the one legged pilot as he had rushed forward with the Chilean Ski Team to arrive in Bariloche quickly as he was a ski race official, President of the German Ski Club. The Chileans were told his club was off limits as it was well known the tables in the living room there featured mostly booklets printed by the German SS featuring picturings of killings of the non German enemies: Poles, Russians, Bulgarians, Serbs.

Mengele was arriving in Bariloche according to my Israeli friends at Portillo who were also on their way to capture Mengele by camping out in the rainy-snowy Patagonia winter. This would be very challenging to them as Israel is a desert country where Jesus and His Disciples were rarely engulfed in Seattle like rain and snow. In my first week in Argentina it decided to snow four feet and then rain for a week and melt it all. Then it changed back to snow then to rain.

The houses in Bariloche and Villa Angostura and San Martin de Los Andes all had excellent roofs and well stocked metal stoves. In those early years they added coal at night just like in New Hampshire sixty years ago.

Mengele had heard about extradition papers for war crimes signed by West Germany for his arrest and sold his carpenter shop in Olivos, a suburb of Buenos Aires two weeks before the Israeli team which kidnapped Eichmann arrived to abduct him as a second target. Mengele eluded them all and fled to Asuncion, Paraguay where he lived in a nice German chalet.

West Germany learned of his whereabouts and signed extradition papers sent to Paraguay so Mengele soon traveled to Brazil. En route he managed to steal some identification papers off some resident with a German last name whose picture looked amazingly similar to his own. His family in Germany kept sending him dividends from the family trust fund so he never quite ran out of money but was close to that when he met a friendly German Brazilian couple near Sao Paulo but in the highlands. The man went off to the city to work every week. Mengele stayed home and screwed his wife. This was where Mengele went between trips to Bariloche yearly to do ice climbing in Bariloche.

The Mengele I saw in Bariloche was definitely this cornered animal of a man fighting on the run hunted by thirty governments and the relatives of six million dead Jews. Of course there were those who didn't really care about finding such a monster and were hoping just the opposite.

I was riding up the lift with an Argentine who pointed at the skier below us doing stem Christies and told me that one is Mengele! I was a young ambitious ski racer and although I found this all intriguing about Mengele I was by now hoping not to meet him as well.

Mengele had escaped capture in Germany because his two grandparents born in New York were possibly not even German and so the SS had not given him the Tattoo of Racial Purity which the Allies were looking for on all the arms of every captured German at the end of World War Two.

General Dwight David Eisenhower the U.S. General of all combined Allied Operations ordered every former German SS officer to be interred in the very same concentration camps they had exterminated the Jews and Untermenschen. Then Dwight David Eisenhower failed to send these German prisoners any food so the starved to death in three weeks.

Mengele of course was never captured and the body of this man whose identification papers he used was dug up in Brazil near where he had died of a heart attack after being rescued from drowning from an undertow while swimming by his German friend (whose wife he screwed) It turned out to be Mangele. He had eluded everyone but the ocean itself and died there in 1971

Heaven is a community

I realize now that I would have been a clerk if I had stayed in my small mid-western town. I might even have been a loan officer at the bank in good standing within my community had I not left to find success out in the woeful world.

So I flew home to my small town and driving from the small airport into town I noticed the road was covered in fine green grass. Phyllis said,

"We haven't had many visitors here in quite a while" she replied which made me laugh and feel at home which I hadn't felt in such a very, very long time.

Then I noticed there were some very small building lots for sale but all were like front yards of existing houses.

"I wouldn;t want to block anyone's view of the fine young policeman driving by offering security"

So Phyllis drove me downtown to see the magistrate or judge so I should present my case why I would want to resettle here in this small town in these great plains where everyone loves each other.

"The sun never sets here" She went on to say adding, "Because God is our light thus we never worry about anything at all and we are free to pray all day and what we ask for is eternal peace and no war since we don't want our children to be drafted like you were to go and fight the godless Bolsheviks"

"Oh that now all makes sense to me now" I replied with my new deeper understanding of this small community in this lovely setting.

I never should have left in the first place therefore I petition my God for forgiveness as I am joyful I will need not pay my debt in full...

St. Littleton

For the kingdom of heaven is like an unhappy man living in a small tiny town.

It's more imperative that we focus on and appreciate what we have round him and criticize everyone and everything he sees,

So he exclaims,

"What a wretched little town this is, so very small, and everyone here is a loser!"

It is his own shortsightedness for belittling his tiny town.

It would be better for him to rename his tiny town "St. Littleton"

Because every street corner is full of potential Saints.

Such a rotten world we live in if we think it so

Yet in the eyes of God it is His Perfection and His Plan

That we rise up and overcome to be the heroes He wants us to be.

We are all potentially His Saints in the making through His Grace

We are reformed only by trial and tribulation.

Thus we each fight a personal Armageddon daily!

My brother and sister Saints now I behold your struggles,

If I were only better able to discern and see your Saintliness in the making

Then I might become a happier man and be more gleeful and Saintly.

"Oh, my dear Saintly brothers and sisters, how I empathize with your mundane daily struggles,

In the final Day we shall all be brothers and rise together to meet God our wonderful Creator

Such great joy will this be and I am now confident in everyone I meet that he or she is sent by you, God, to help me fulfill my role in Your Grand Plan

What God has ordained for us here and now

Rather than upon what we don't have though we might want more

The Wild West has won and the Toddler Is Reinstalled, copyright 2020 Duncan Cullman

5:18 AM

The Wild West Gun Show has reinstalled the Toddler to four more years during which the United States will pursue rampant unchecked capitalism and unchecked carbon emissions. The losers of this race are the American Medical Association which wanted to impose its own form of dictatorship and the minority races who thrive more when Washington is more generous with foodstamps and Negro Education.

How this became possible is largely the fault of mumbling Joe Biden who was unintelligible through his mask. His entire career was spent espousing any cause that would be opposite of Republicans while he and his son indulged in minor corruption themselves. In his mystical hypocrisy he chose his vice president to accommodate the left wing of his party the Bernie-ites.

It appears she was the wrong choice to attract the honky tonk disaffectionados of Dixie and the Wild West who would probably prefer a Conservative Southern Democrat with a twang.

Therefore the movement to install "Any Functioning Adult" has taken a complete defeat enabling the hysterical toddler to reinstate his cause of White Power and climate destruction. The big losers are half the world's species both plant and animal whose extinction is now surely accelerated as is the extinction of homo sapiens as well. The Trumpet existentialists intend to live it up while they are still alive and disregard the environmental mess they are handing to their own grandchildren.

Congratulations to "Toddler-in-Chief" and his merry followers whose optimism has been more dazzling in these Pandemic Moments of Glum and Despair" with Dr. Fauci and the WHO.

As for us we will go skiing as the total shutdown will be avoided while coal burns furiously so there will now be even fewer years remaining with snow and ice on this planet. We may see reverberations around the world for our nonconformity to scientific wisdom but bigger business will prevail as usual

Near to me

Call on the Lord while He is near

When you are lost or before you become lost look for a beacon

Because the Lord alone is my light and salvation

On the open sea where waves crash against my boat in darkness

I do not know how near to me Leviathan that serpent lurks beneath

If I do not pray then surely I am lost with no light to save me no moon no stars

The sun itself may not rise on my tomorrow if I cannot pass this night in prayer

What will become of me and who will there be who still remembers me

"O yes we knew him too bad he fell off his high castle wall thinking himself indestructible

Did he think he was Donald Trump or something like that?

Therefore call on the Lord well before you are a Humpty
Dumpty

All the king's horses and all the king's men couldn't put
Humpty back together

Again I pray save me my Lord from such catastrophe
be my Savior

Die on a cross for me that I taste not death but rise with
you into your kingdom

To be in that room you have prepared for me where I
will be safe forever

For you have set a table before me in the presence of
my enemies

You are near to me my breastplate of armour my shield
and buckler

I will not fear though I walk through the valley of death
because you are with me

Your anointed child who shall proclaim your greatness
forever who shall sing hymns

Let my song reverberate in the hills let my laughter
continue with friends

Let us sup together those of my own understanding
who earnestly pray

Bring us together as a nation of angels as a congregation
of good

We are righteously calling your name in this darkness
see us

Look down upon us have mercy that we may one day
dwell with you in Sion

What are bears doing in Santiago?

What are bears doing in Santiago?

Bears eat berries.

Bears love honey.

When it's cold, Bears hibernate.

Then they wake up hungry!

What's all that noise? ask the curious bears.

There's A city down there in all that smog and noise

Many garbage cans surrounded by barking dogs

The dogs stop barking when the warm sun rises to warm the sidewalk.

Now that the dogs are asleep we can go to Santiago, say the bears

We don't have wallets so nobody can rob us the subway

We don't have backpacks so nobody can pick through them while we walk

We don't have passports so they don't think we're rich gringo tourists

What do we need taxis for? proclaim the bears

We're bears! We go where we want to!

The policeman lets us cross the street.

The cars stop and people stare at us.

The signs all say,

Don't feed the bears(or the dogs!)

The grocery man throws oranges at us and runs away

We want the blueberries and look some peanuts

Bears eat anything at all and everything, say the passing
schoolchildren!

Run says their teacher, run children run

We're not scared of bears say the children

(Fear is something they teach us in school)

We're not afraid either say the hungry bears

Look the supermarket shelves are empty,

Bears don't even carry credit cards

Dogs have woken up now from all this commotion

Dogs are barking wildly in the street

Let's go home say the bears

Follow that bus that says San Jose de Maipo says Papa
Bear

Yes that's the bus says Mama Bear

The bus driver sees the bears, stops the bus and runs
to the subway

Board the bus all my cubbies says Papa Bear

Mama Bear didn't lose her license she can drive

All the bears go home to Cajon de maipo where they
climb,

Where they climb some more up and up

Into the mighty Andes Mountains.

There are no bears in Chile says a policeman!(he doesn't
understand climate change)

We know better. We are the bears

More of Jimmy On The Mountain

"Any day you can wake up in America and make a cup of coffee, even if you have no money at all, is a very good day indeed!" That is what Jimmy Thompson always said with a wide grin. Sometimes he would roll a joint and we would smoke one or two puffs of that stuff too then he would extinguish it and save what was left for just before he went to sleep.

He did have nightmares too and would wake up screaming thinking he was back there in "Nam", Vietnam in that battle that almost ended his life. A great big guy, his friend, took a bullet or two and fell on top of him dead. It saved his life at least for that very moment when the battle broke out. The 101rst had walked into a horseshoe shaped ambush with the NVR, North Vietnsmese regulars coming out of holes in the ground to catch the Americans in a deadly crossfire. Somehow, perhaps when darkness ensued, Jimmy managed to crawl under a tree which had been hit by a mortar so of course there was no tree left but a big dislodged root system with a hole under it. He continued to play dead. Only one other American was still alive in his vicinity and they could hear the NVR doing a body count of the Americans shooting anyone who was still alive. First light ensued and those NVR's in their pajamas were getting really close so they had to start shooting their very last magazines.

Luckily at that moment U.S. Navy Warthogs swooped down a dropped napalm narrowly missing them. There were the screams of those being roasted in burning plastic and the NVR that were still alive ran away.

Jimmy was Medevaced, evacuated by helicopter as his wounds were severe. He woke up in a Hospital Ship and then was flown back to the United States where he gave some lectures to green recruits about to be shipped out over there to "Nam". At least he now had hot coffee. After two months of this despite being constantly recruited to re-up which is re-enlist he fought off the temptation which for him was not so tempting at all. He had almost been killed and everyone in his platoon of over one hundred had been killed except for seven of them. He felt very good to be alive. He was relishing every good cup of hot coffee even if there was no cream or sugar. He was discharged and returned to his mother Rita's house in North Conway, New Hampshire. You can get there by bus from Boston in about five hours back then. Coming back to placid little New Hampshire was like returning to Fairy Land or Walt Disney with Mickey Mouse. People he met in the streets were mostly war protestors and very few thanked him for his service. These people whether they were for or against the war had almost no concept of total war other than Hogan's Heroes or Gomer Pyle. There were still some documentaries of Iwo Jima from WWII with the Marines using flamethrowers scalding everyone but until you can smell burning flesh and possibly your own you don't have any idea that you are totally expendable. The U.S. Military Industrial Complex WANTS YOU for cannon fodder.

So Jimmy and his young wife Cindy and their daughter Valerie headed for Taos, New Mexico to go live with the Indians. Many of those Indians had served in various wars as it was their opportunity to get a job and see the world plus receive the G.I. Bill and a few even went to college where they studied mostly agriculture or forestry. A few became lawyers and politicians. All the money in New Mexico is the Bank of Texas which managed to buy most of the farms in Eastern New Mexico leaving just the badlands and some hills in Western New Mexico to the Spanish and or Indians who inter marry, it is true. All the pure Indians, Navahos, Commanche and Apaches had mostly died of smallpox.

Jimmy liked it there in New Mexico living among some hippie communes until war broke out with some local badass Spanish who began shooting at them killing a few. The Sihks then bought a machine gun and fired back at the native Mexican Spanish-Indian mix badasses. Cindy had not been to war and was uneasy and left for Tamworth, New Hampshire to be with her mother. Me and Jimmy who I had originally met at Joe Jones ski shop in North Conway where he was a salesman, we hitchhiked to Pilar to play cards because we had no money at all and Jimmy thought he could win a few dollars if our hosts got very drunk late into the night. Jimmy won forty dollars and we were camping out with a guest host when our gracious hosts began

taking pot shots at us at six o'clock in the morning.
Bang. Bang. Bang.

"That means we are supposed to leave!" said Jimmy
with a wide smile again adding,

"No time for coffee here this morning, we'll hitch to
Taos and buy some on the Plaza. We had some money
and we'd get some "Huevos Rancheros "with flour
tortillas and Chili Verde(green sauce).

Jimmy told me he had once been camping in the
mountains here with Charles Manson who had a gang.
Some young little hippies overdosed possibly on heroin
or cocaine. Rather than call the police the Manson
gang just threw the dead bodies on the bonfire. That
took care of that. Then the Mansons moved to Nevada
and California to eventually kill a bunch of movie stars
including Sharon Tate at her pool in Beverly Hills.
What was left out of that story was that Richard Nixon
had authorized with covert money the manufacture of
"Jacob's Ladder" a type of LSD for use by the American
military to use in battle and totally become psychotic
and enjoy killing with no remorse whatsoever. There
were laboratories funded by our own government all over
the United States of America giving this stuff away at
discount prices to any young or old hippy wanting to
be a guinea pig for experimentation.

Jimmy then brought his Ecuadorian girlfriend to
Silverton, Colorado where I had bought a mining claim
and had been host to a handful of college graduate
hippies from Ohio who had now run off to new
adventures, Shawn was her name as she had at least one
gringo parent. She made chipettes which were between

pancakes and tortillas but very delicious. Jimmy made his coffee while I attended the fire adding dry sticks or the stove adding chopped fallen branches. We had a view of twin peaks over thirteen thousand feet. We were in my cabins that were beyond rustic on a mining claim eleven miles from town all uphill to this cabin site at eleven thousand nine hundred forty feet on the side of Bonita Peak.

I am not sure why we ever left but Shawn probably wanted to take a bath in town. We ran for water up there to nearby streams but had no running water to speak of.

Jimmy went to Washington, D.C. to teach many others the great lessons he had learned as I was not the best of students. He died there in 2010 among other Vietnam War Veterans and a whole flock of very devoted friends I am sure

Franny on Mount Everest

Let us remember that it was the intensity with which we lived and be remembered for that rather than for longevity. All of the preceding because life is but five deep breaths not more. We are like the grass that grows before noon and wilts all too soon when the sun does zenith overhead.

Franny was my friend who perhaps loved more my dog Helga than me at first. She invited us over for dinner being delighted to cook something delicious for my dear dog Helga who took a very kind fancy to all females as they were indeed her own sex.

Franny had been raised in Columbia, Missouri which is a slightly northern outpost of Dixie between Kansas City and St Louis. Her father was a professor there at the University of Missouri. I had gone there once in my younger days to be turned down in love by a beautiful young blond actress with very Saxon features.

Now being older and wiser though reeling in pain and suffering from a sudden divorce with children, I had started a new job as ski instructor in the prestigious western ski resort, Telluride, Colorado.

Franny asked me just exactly how I made love which was puzzling to her as her boss, Johnny Stevens, had informed her that I must be gay. I began to try to explain but it was no use and much easier to follow her leads and not contradict her in any way;and soon I was rubbing her back for her after the very pleasant dinner with some wine She had no objections nor any fear of me, a gay man understandably. Her buttocks which cried out for attention and massage were perhaps the most amazing I had ever encountered, bonny hot crossed buns indeed She had climbed Mount Kendall 13,455 feet high in nearby Silverton in an hour and twenty minutes setting a new record for that competition every summer. I doubt anyone has since broken it.

Her passion aside from skiing was evidently hiking high up the sides of the Rocky Mountains and other lofty mountains. Soon she would travel to Russia to climb Mt Stalin which has been renamed something else but is still the same height 25,091. There she would fall in love with her guide, the Russian climber Antsiuev whose partner the previous year had perished on Mount Everest guiding too many inexperienced climbers up there to all their deaths for a great sum of money he would not live to spend.

The two of them, Franny and Antsiev married and he built her a house near Telluride which they then mortgaged to finance their climbing adventure up Mount Everest. She, at last minute, invited me to her new home, perhaps to see them off or perhaps because she not only loved her new husband but feared him as well. Unfortunately, I declined being both busy and absurdly jealous. Off they traveled in spite of her small son's nightmare that they would be lost in a snowstorm on top of a very high mountain.

I was in a breakfast cafe in Glenwood Springs, Colorado a few months later while my dog Helga waited for me patiently in the car outside for all the best scraps I might bring her.

Some news on the television about an American hiker who had just climbed Mount Everest without oxygen and had been the very first woman ever to do that and her name was something strange, some Russian sounding name. Unfortunately she and her husband had tried to set up their tent on the descent in 100 mile per hour winds but it had been blown away so they continued down by foot too rapidly to the twenty thousand foot level but she had gotten the bends so he wandered off to find help. They had been up there above sixteen thousand feet over a month acclimatizing so as to make an ascent without oxygen. Unfortunately she was found near death and he went insane and wandered off somewhere disappearing perhaps into a crevasse.

I had heard enough and I rushed to buy a newspaper or two and discovered to my horror and disappointment it was indeed my Franny, my teammate in the Telluride Governor's Cup ski competition which our team including Colorado's own governor Romer had won prestigiously the year before.(I had beaten Franz Klammer by .1 seconds for fastest time as well)

I went to the Memorial service held for her where her first husband and young son were in attendance and we all cried many tears for her and maybe ourselves as well.

Years have passed by and many more of my friends and former ladies of renown have likewise passed as well.

Let us remember them dearly not how they all died but how each one lived exuberantly and passionately they sprang up before us like shining flowers in a sunlit field in splendid colors each one given exceptional beauty and grace by God alone.

I want to thank God also for my own life which has been blessed meeting so many very special gifted people, each person had a very important impact on my own life as ordained by our Lord and Creator to bring great joy into this world.

It shall not matter that we face world wars or pandemics threatening us with gloom and doom because we are all shining flowers like Franny each and every one of us is very special to God in both this life and hereafter.

There is great adversity in this world and suffering but it is there in order for us to not be spineless wimps but courageous heroes because that is what God wants for us- that we each reach our great summit like Franny on Mount Everest. Thank you, God for creating Franny to show us the way up, the way up there to that lofty summit of your grace and eternal love for us- that we may now love each other more deeply, Franny was barely alive when some American climbers said they stumbled upon her and she said,

"I'm an American. Can you help me?"

A storm was coming in and the climbers had to abandon her, they said. Seven years later they returned because of their conconscience to find her still there frozen in the snow with a smile on her face. They called her "Sleeping Beauty" when they had first found her seven years before. Now they pulled her body into a more remote location and draped an American Flag over her held down by some rocks. Franny is still there on Mount Everest.

"Young Pro Ski Racer"
Hard Fast Life in the Rockies

I was a young pro ski racer with the International Ski Racers Association when I traveled to Aspen, Colorado in 1972. I was ranked tenth overall and sixth in slalom with winnings of $6,500 which was more than enough to buy a cheeseburger and beer special at Pinocchio's Restaurant where the waitresses wore short skirts and low cut blouses for big tips and mine had big ones and a friendly smile, probably from drinking from a flask on the job but that didn't matter to me at all.

She had auburn reddish hair and told me her mother was Swedish from Stockholm (actually more Danish). This was close enough for me and going home to her trailer because I was homeless: this was heaven and she was the goddess herself though possibly a drinker, was I to complain?

Young pro ski racers or young amateur ski racer was really a title given to all of us who loved the sport of skiing back then. There was no freestyle and no snowboarding, and no super giant slalom, just three alpine events and three gold medals every four years in the Olympics which were televised. It was the sport of rich white children who went on family vacations including Christmas to snow covered hills where the children mostly skied and the adults mostly got drunk and told wild stories.

Actually it was the year before in 1971 when I first met Phyllis Garrett whose parents had moved from Indiana to Grand Junction. My homeless winter wandering separated us seasonally because I still lived in New Hampshire but wanted to live in the west like my rich friend John Stirling whose parents had just died leaving him four million dollars, including land in Florida, apartments in California, over a hundred acres on Missouri Heights in Carbondale, Colorado and a very small cabin with no plumbing in Aspen where the ski industry was now thriving and tearing up the old wooden sidewalks of it's past mining era and replacing them with concrete, even paving the once mud streets. That was real western clay mud, at least five pounds stuck under each boot sole.

I managed to tip my waitress a hundred dollar bill which is like a few thousand dollars now. She was a saloon gal and we moved together to Telluride in 1974 where I finally landed a job, racing director, and she was a cocktail waitress at the former brothel at the east end of town where they even gave her free drinks and kept her there till 1 am or later. I was not terribly happy about it and disappeared into the Sheraton Hotel for five days with Franny. Phyllis was not happy about that maneuver either. Of course I managed to ski every day at my job as I was the Nastar Pacesetter. Ski Racing was the big show back then and freestylers were all pot smoking hippy liberals who ate granola and grew beards living in Volkswagen buses.

I soon had nowhere to live without Phyllis's generous rent support and I brought home Chandler to my comfy metal house with no heat, someone had given me a key to it as the owner was away. We froze together one long night with a few in between not sweaty flashes.

After building a pro jump for my racecourse with the ski area chainsaw on the Nastar race hill, the ski area was fined $1,000 dollars by the U.S. Forest Service. I was not going to be rehired, at least they let me know in Aptil. My pay had been very meager indeed as I was considered crazy enough and a fool skier to accept carpenter wages, my own terms. I had left home young with no college but managed to gain a berth on the U.S. Ski Team by winning the Junior Nationals GS though only runner-up in the Downhill. Bob Beattie, the U.S. Ski Coach now became my parental overseer, a job he was decidedly not too thrilled with after interviewing me he realized I didn't have any maturity whatsoever, that I was mostly a young hound after naked young ladies I did occasionally catch ones my own age, this is an event that lasts only a very few years before reality sets in and finances overcome hormones.

Phyllis's mother chain smoked cigars and pipes, anything she could get her hands on especially after work at her home where she interviewed me as a ditch digger and was not very terribly impressed.

So Phyllis started working for the Post Office, a very respectable job her parents bent over backward on her behalf but she still loved alcohol and was late to work more than once. So after I found her and took her binge drinking with my friends from Silverton who had wandered in there from various parts of the world as refugees to local bars that had instructed them about a young pro ski racer that lived at 12,600 feet above Gladstone who might provide quarters for them.

To shorten the story we loaded Phyllis into my car from the sidewalk where she passed out cold and away we drove into the night back up to 12,600 feet elevation where it sometimes doesn't snow in August but sleets hail instead.

Phyllis's mother was ballistic but her father was understanding. She decided to ditch me one evening for Nick Nohava, an ex-convict until she found out about him. She moved into Silverton proper and took a job with some Navaho who's store sold turquoise.

I was very sad to lose Phyllis but really the bottle was destroying her. She went home to never be forgiven by her smoking mother while her two sisters moved out successfully, Ingrid and Christine. Then she went to Alcoholics Anonymous and met some heroin addicts who had gone cold turkey because of the New Life Assembly of God. Jesus proceeded to save them all while they recruited lost rich hippy children defrocking them of their trust funds and family inheritances for good cause which became an EXODUS TO TEXAS.

I am no longer a young ski racer. I sold my mining claim in Silverton due to thyroid failure quite possibly triggered by drinking spring water for dishes only that my fellow mom-comrades brought from the nearby Lead Carbonate Mine, abandoned.

I sent some letters to Texas after visiting Phyllis once in Paonia with my ski friend Racer Rob Mulrenan who was impressed with her,

"Well, Doctor," he called me and said, "You have good taste. She has les Grand Tetons" he smiled in a whisper. We were all becoming middle age ski bums which is not such a glorious profession when the snow melts in May.

I never heard one thing from Phyllis except she did RETURN TO SENDER my Christmas in July parcel I sent her from Lake City, Colorado.

There was a note attached, something to the effect, "I am all done with you!"

Twelve years after Phyllis died, I saw an obituary for us all on <u>ancestry.com</u>

"She was a well respected member of the community and her church in West, Texas. She has gone to the angels now to be one of them."

We are looking forward to hanging stars with her in heaven, Saint Phyllis. Her God given gift was animal husbandry. She preached the Good News of Salvation to farm animals which immediately fell in love and copulated creating abundance.

She fell in love and married a Dutchman with blond hair who sailed off somewhere. She leaves behind a son, Peter, two sisters and a dog and three cats and several thousand farm animals deeply in love.

All you Bedouins out there wandering over the hills

(like skiers) looking for your stray animals, come home to your Father (Family vacation skiing) and hear the Word of God, that He is Good For in the beginning there was God....

My friend is a dog named Rusio

My friend is a dog named Rusio

He lives in a country called Chile

Which is shaped roughly like a strand of spaghetti

In the north it is very dry and is a desert

In the south of Chile it rains alot where Rusio lives in Villarica.

Sometimes in winter it snows in Chile but usually in the high Andes Mountains

But sometimes it snows down low in the towns.

No one knows where Rusio came from, only Rusio

Just a year ago today he arrived in town probably he was abandoned by an irresponsible bad owner

He was discovered first by one nearly dawn tourist who noticed the hungry dog and went to the nearby market to buy him some dog food and snacks

The tourist went to sleep very sad that night because he was worrying about his new friend the dog named Rusio.

Rusio was a named picked for the dog by various local

shopkeepers because he was a blond short haired dog so they gave him a name that means Russian.

Rusio had seems to have a friend who is another dog named Oranginho who is colored like an orange(and probably a Chinese Chow dog). Oranginho follows Rusio everywhere they run side by side. Oranginho wants to know where Rusio is getting his food.

Someone has been feeding Rusio steak and roast beef. Is it the lady Madelyn in Artes Sur who sells wool hats and socks? Or is it the lady Michelle who sells wooden bowls? She came here from France for love and married but her husband passed away. Or is it Giovanni the cook at Balganez Restaurant where business is slow in winter season? Or is it that same tourist who eats kuchen tortas at Kuchenladen with his afternoon tea?

Because a cloud of sweet smelling gas follows Rusio wherever he goes. That is why Oranginho follows him everywhere. He wants to be so popular like Rusio who seemingly has friends everywhere all over the town but growls now at Oranginho to please stand out of his way and not smother him.

Who for instance has bought Rusio the new pea green leather collar with dangling miniature milkbones? Everyone loves Rusio even though he has no home but just wanders around the entire town.

Let's see if we can find Rusio a nice home somewhere where he can be warm and not starving where no cars will run him over in the street!

He is my friend Rusio and he is a dog! Bring him home someone please! And bring me home too, I am a homeless person named Agostino. We all need to be loved and find a home to shield us from the storms!

BEARS VISIT SANTIAGO,
a children's book

"What are bears doing in Santiago?"

Bears eat berries.

Bears love honey.

When its cold, Bears hibernate.

Then they wake up hungry!

"What's all that noise?" ask the curious bears.

"There's a city down there in all that smog and noise!"

"Many garbage cans surrounded by barking dogs!"

The dogs stop barking when the warm sun rises to warm the sidewalk.

"Now that the dogs are asleep we can go to Santiago", say the bears

"We don't have wallets so nobody can rob us the subway"

"We don't have backpacks so nobody can pick through them while we walk"

"We don't have passports so they won't think we're rich gringo tourists"

"What do we need taxis for?" proclaim the bears

"We are bears! We go where we want to!"

The policeman lets us cross the street.

The cars stop and people stare at us.

The signs all say,

"Don't feed the bears!"

The grocery man throws oranges at us and runs away

"We want the blueberries and look some peanuts!"

"Bears eat anything at all and everything," say the passing schoolchildren!

"Run says their teacher, run children run!"

"We're not scared of bears," say the children

(Fear is something they accidentally taught us in school)

"We're not afraid either!", say the hungry bears

"Look, the supermarket shelves are empty,."

Bears don't even carry credit cards

Dogs have woken up now from all this commotion

Dogs are barking wildly in the street

"Let's go home," say the bears.

"Follow that bus that says San Jose de Maipo," says Papa Bear

"Yes that's the bus," says Mama Bear

The bus driver sees the bears, stops the bus and runs to the subway

"Board the bus all my cubbies!" says Papa Bear.

"Mama Bear didn't lose her license she can drive!"

All the bears go home to Cajon de Maipo where they climb,

Where they climb some more up and up

Into the mighty Andes Mountains.

"There are no bears in Chile!" says a policeman!(he doesn't understand climate change)

Mrs Stone and the Mountain Shaped like a Volcano

There was a guy John Roth who came to Silverton and bought the Grand Imperial Hotel, a relic of the turn of the century not this one but the last, 1900.

It was in a sad state of affairs but John Roth had either money or credit, his Anglo-Saxon ancestors going back to the American Revolution and George Washington. He had both. Therefore it was restored. I may even have worked there a day or two as a laborer with none of the necessary skills I was let go, fired. It was hard not to come back to the place, its bar out of the late eighteen hundreds in those days when gold and silver were discovered in great abundance in Colorado, an inhospitable state with winter nightime temperatures in the mountains of about thirty below aero in January. The erected wooden shacks housing the miners had no insulation in the walls nor foundations but coal was in abundance finally brought in by the narrow gauge railroad from Durango although Red Mountain had a railroad from Ouray and the north where Somerset had coal so did Hesperus to the west of Durango, the home terminal of the Silverton Galloping Goose which defied avalanches and hailstorms to ferry its passengers and cargo to Silverton.

About ninety years later a hairdresser from New York City arrived with her slightly younger husband who served more as her valet. She did recently have a dream in New York of acquiring vast wealth and she went to her good friend the fortune teller who confirmed her intuitions that in a high mountain in Colorado out west, shaped like a volcano, near Silverton she would discover a vein of Gold leading straight down into Middle Earth itself, unmeasurable wealth like the Orient itself like all the Incas and Pizarro combined. She sold her salon and managed to borrow money from investor-speculators and pulled her husband by the ear across the Great Plains as well to look at the spectacular Rocky Mountains to see a mountain shaped like a volcano near Silverton. There it was. She spotted it and went to the local real estate broker feigning to buy a large house on main street which she did and then adding that she didn't know what to do with the rest of her very large sum of money.

"Well, you might speculate in patented mining claims and wait for the price of gold to come back up!" offered the realtor who thought of her as some Eastern fool. Everyone knew FDR took America off the gold standard and ever since mining had gone to hell. Now there was this woman who seemingly wanted to go to hell with it?

"Yes that's such a pretty mountain and my husband can build me a summer home up there from all those large spruce trees. Are they really over two hundred years old?" She bought every available mining claim on that thirteen thousand peak both patented and unpatented. The realtor was beginning to suspect something but what did he care as his commissions were even larger on mining claims.

My Ohio friends who were students recently at Ohio State but had hitchhiked into town ato drink beer at The Grand Imperial Hotel then lived at my cabins as guests for several months with no employment almost none at all. They went to town for beer and met some very exquisite lady with a valet husband she pulled around by his ascot. This lady and her husband were wearing cowboy hats of the best quality but were obviously New Yorkers with no horses in sight anywhere but there was a very large four wheel drive Land Cruiser outside. the lady promptly hired them both plus a Caterpillar driver who would bulldoze her a road to that summit of her golden mountain,

"Oh isn't it beautiful!" she exclaimed looking at the majestic mountain but more at the gold inside of it. Off they all drove and the bulldozer made it all the way up there pulling two sledges, one a luxury trailer, the finest money could buy and the other exactly the opposite, a quarters for the help with a coal burning wood stove but not being so well made it suffered some damage on the long trip up there so that there were several cracks in the walls that needed to be stuffed with rags. Also its roof leaked. The weather still wasn't too bad at the end of October but then a howling wind came which was the advent of winter and it soon snowed, snowed and kept snowing while the wind did not abate at all.

Mts. Stone dressed in her minks barking the orders for her motley crew of two, my friends Nick and Gus,

"Dig, dig, dig straight down. Use those picks. Here

my husband will bring the dynamite. Bang. Bang!"
They were on their way to China or hell whichever
might appear first. Meanwhile at the bottom of the
mountain the bulldozer slid in all that snow flipping
over killing its driver. They were now cut off on top of
that peak with enough supplies for the Chinese Army
if they should discover it.

Of course it turned out there was no gold and my
friends were waiting to get their final paycheck when
Mrs. Stone slipped out of town one 3 A.M. never to
be seen again with creditors looking for her from coast
to coast. Rumor had it she made it to San Francisco to
open a brothel or something. All these are just rumors
as this entire story was made up by Nick and Gus for
me to believe. However the bulldozer driver did die
unfortunately. life is hard in the Rockies and Silverton
was no exception.

Gus went off to Pilar, New Mexico with Nick and
Jimmy and they cultivated marijuana but not Jimmy
who left for New Hampshire and Washington, D.C.

They were about to reap a very large harvest when
Gus saw Mount Zion and God who told him to throw
his portion of the marijuana in the Rio Grande River
across the street. Nick ran off with his share to sell it to
Mrs, Stone or whoever might buy it and wasn't heard
from as he probably soon got free room and boarded
up the river somewhere. Gus after seeing Jesus and
the Angels returned to Toledo to be a good Catholic
marry and raise a family and be saintly. Mrs. Stone it
was rumored died shortly thereafter so her creditors got
burned in hell as they say.

The Monastic Life at St. Bernard's Monastery Ski Area

The Monastery St. Bernard

After exploring south and west in the land of more sun and higher mountains I purchased for two thousand nine hundred ninety nine dollars a patented mining claim entitled Bastile at eleven thousand eight hundred fifty feet altitude, roughly twice the altitude of Mt Washington, New Hampshire;and thereupon after selling my original one acre of land in Twin Mountain, New Hampshire in order to complete the sale with a five thousand mile drive in an orange Datsun hallucinating most of the way just from exhaustion, I henceforce began to build a monstrous ten by ten foot cabin with some Ohio hitchikers I had picked up on the way west:most notably Ken Saffranski who insisted on picking up his girlfriend Dianne Stauder who was pleased with herself to find a ride in any direction after having flunked out of Ohio State her sophomore year due to excessive drinking drugs and wild sex orgies. She proceeded to be so happy she insisted on doing both of us and I being sloppy seconds managed to bring her to an unrivaled climax thereupon she became my girlfriend for almost two years.

I knew Mynx might not be too thrilled about my new companion as Mynx had been up there first to the "Monastery" we called it. But Mynx was preoccupied in distant adventures with her Daddy sailing the Atlantic.

Hank Dane and later his girlfriend Michelle Spanos would come visit from Sugar Hill and Indian Head Resort in Franconia Notch. Then Safransky brought his college mate Gus Campagna who found in a bar some Nick Nohava whose last name was an alias as Indiana wanted him but he couldn't go back there! Like the song definitely.

We would drive to town, buy rice, potatoes bullets and beer more beer. The monks seemed to have a passion more for beer and less for brewing wine which was too time consuming. We were so busy playing croquet, horseshoes, skiing on summer snow and inviting every character we could find in Silverton and nationwide to come visit eleven thousand nine hundred feet overnight then climb the grassy ridge to Bonita Peak thirteen thousand two hundred feet. Mynx saved my life in a rainstorm on the far side of the mountain where we had gone on a ski adventure scantily clad in tee shirts when she produced out of a plastic mini-jar three matches of which the third was successful in starting a bonfire. But Mynx was history now. New adventurers arrived from France with indescribable expressions on their faces as they had expected a full hostel with running water.

"Oh we run on over there to the stream for our water!" explained Gus to the awestruck travelers who replied,

"This is not a hostel how did you get a license, in France it is very difficult?"

"Well we are in the process of building the hostel" I pointed to the site seventy yards distant where our fourth building was under construction.

Luckily the Frenchmen and their woman had brought some acid LSD and then there was a nonstop party into the next day so they had fun but departed and we lost our license oh well.

Nick and Gus went to work for Mrs Stone a hairdresser from Manhattan who bought a mountaintop of mining claims on the advice of her distant fortune teller who told her to dig straight down into the center of the earth and find rare gems. She had propane heat in her luxurious abode at thirteen thousand four hundred feet while Nick and Gus claimed they shivered sleeping in some kind of cave up there. The bulldozer driver lost his life maintain her road while her husband was very understanding as it was all her money anyway...

Nick and Gus came back to the Monastery after she failed to pay them, another Silverton, Colorado mining story.

So we rescued Phyllis a telephone operator in Grand Junction from her job she hated anyway. She was struggling with her tendency toward alcoholism but at the Monastery alcohol was the alleviant to boredom so she fell off the wagon then moved into town with an Indian selling turquoise then joined a religious cult found God and moved to Texas.

So Nick and Gus went with my good friend from North Conway Jimmy Thompson to Taos where they learned the Hemp farming business and soon produced a few tons for distribution. Thereupon Gus remembered his religious commitments to the Monastery and envisioned God Jesus who told him to throw his portion of the righteous weed into the Rio Grande River which He did and so was saved. Of course Nick flipped out grabbed what he could and departed for the drug trade never to be seen again except perhaps by Jesus Himself perhaps at the Gate.

Dianne too found a higher calling and flew away on a jet plane to Ireland where she fell in love married had two children and proceeded to love mostly "Men of the Sea". At least Gus is my distant friend on facebook to this day and he is in contact with her and her sister who after using my ski poles left them at the ski area. Jimmy Thompson told me all his war stories so I wrote them down, his hiding under a blasted tree as his position was overrun by North Vietnamese Regulars. He had smoked a lot of the righteous weed and was suffering some paranoia with his post traumatic stress. Poor baby. Yes we all are poor babies way down deep inside like Led Zeppelin the song.

The Monastery was sold to an aspiring monk from Telluride for fifteen thousand dollars as unfortunately we had all grown up and moved elsewhere. Jesus, I am sure, follows us everywhere still I hope-

My Brother Graham

Finally I will get to see my brother. I saw him almost every day between 1953 and 1961 except for vacations of course. Our parents were not even the same yet we grew up in the same house. We lived under one roof and his mother fed us all, my own father plus her husband, Graham's father. Though sometimes we ate in separate dining quarters we usually got together after meals or to practice baseball at 6AM before school though that crack of the bat and yelling in the backyard upset his sleeping mother or the sleeping neighbors or my sleeping father.

Didn't we get enough sports at school his mother and father wondered? My own father had other things on his mind, namely business and the stock market. Plus where was he going tonight, to which cocktail party to social climb? He spoke softly to me at the breakfast table and explained the world to me from behind his newspaper he was reading, The New York Times.

"I was born into this world to be like my own father who is an aristocrat. It's not our fault that we are rich and other people are poor. We are who we are to become like our own parents not like other people who are different from us. They are the way they are for several generations. If their parents are bums then they are bums, If a man is a house servant than his child is more likely to be a house servant too. Your father is rich so you will probably be too if you learn your lessons in school. You like the outdoors more so maybe you will be an engineer?"

"An F.B.I!" I protested. I liked to dig with my shovel in the backyard. My mountain of dirt was an imaginary ski hill for our favorite toys, stuffed mice from Germany. They were originally manufactured to be bookmarks in Germany but in our back yard each one had a name and an individual personality. They even won ski races like the Olympics for Mice!

Graham's original mouse was so worn from love that it lost all its hair covering and was still shaped like a field mouse but was all the more just brown mouse leather. My mice I always managed to lose. Sometimes they went to school with me.

"What is that thing in your pocket?" Screamed the elderly teacher!

"Oh it's just my fieldmouse!"

"Abhorrent! Put that thing away and don't bring that back to school, understand?"

My father would ask me to show my pet mouse to elderly ladies at our own Jewish family gatherings. I would place the mouse between my thumb and index finger and wiggle it from another finger below. The women would all scream!

Graham knew my technique however his father who had been in the R.A.F. was very strict and wouldn't let him indulge in such nonsense. I had met all his family relatives. They were all English and drank tea from the best tea cups from England or China, Singapore or Mandalay. The men had all been soldiers in the Second World War. They didn't talk about it with the women not to scare them. Sometimes at the beach they told some war stories just amongst themselves and we boys could sometimes listen unless it was grown up talk which pertain more to business and grievances.

I actually spent much more time with Graham's family than with my own as midweek I ate my meals with them in the kitchen. They were our servants but I never looked down on them. Caroline was like my mother now that I had lost my own to the Sanatorium in Great Barrington, Massachusetts. I went there with my father to visit her. I was not allowed inside. The car was very cold but my father probably asked if I could ski on the snow and someone must have said they would babysit me from inside the doorway. It was snowing. I imagined my own mother was watching me and always remembered it that way although she most likely was not. Finally my father came out of the building and I did not even see my mother once. Caroline, my governess, had nothing better to do than to love me as well. She had lost one child in childbirth she later confessed to me and I filled the empty space she had, I became her second child. That was very lucky for me as I was actually adopted of Anglo-Saxon origin so I was most fortunate to be raised proper English with an English accent as the Groves were immigrants from near London; but of course Graham had been born stateside.

Frank or actually Francis was Graham Grove's father's name. He had loaded the ordinances on the

British Spitfires in the air Battle of London which the Germans called Der Blitz. The English were very proud to have beaten the Germans in the War even though it had almost destroyed their empire. They had lost many colonies and lost many ships on the high seas which were now replaced by American Ships. Though they had won the War somehow they had managed to lose the War. They all knew it and it was a sore subject though they had been lucky to emigrate over here where wages were higher they had to take menial jobs like roofing, lawn cutting and carpentry. They really did struggle to make ends meet. They drove English cars, like the miniature Ford to save on gas but the cars broke down and were not entirely reliable.

Frank had been a semi-pro soccer player in England and had broken his leg quite badly preventing him from making the Professional League. It was a bitter disappointment for him but that made him a baker in Caroline's parents pastry shop, I am sure it was really a very splendid place that one. Graham sometimes talked about it and complained that here in America nothing was quite as good as England. I didn't want to hear it as I had never been there and would never go. My father had business in South America where they also drank afternoon tea fifty and a hundred or two years ago but the custom has stopped in these modern times regretfully.

Frank wanted us to play soccer but we didn't have it in our own schools, my private one and his public school just had football and baseball. When my father went away all of Graham's family came to play Cricket in our backyard. The hard wooden ball struck me and gave me a slight bruise. I cried as I was for the most part still a baby though already four feet tall.

So we played baseball the All American sport invented before the Civil War but Frank didn't have that information. Our little league bats were so small Frank used just one hand to hit us fly balls to catch until I ran into the stone wall trying to catch a really high fly. I was knocked unconscious and got a whole week off to rest and recuperate but then we were back out there in the yard.

"Please, Frank, hit us another one!" We cried. Eventually we took turns ourselves with Graham hitting some to me and visa versa. Then Frank took the coaching job with the Masonic Little League Team of Royaton. I had played the previous year with the Kiwanis Team then actually missed a season as I went to South America to sightsee and ski with my father and Mrs. Wing. We had gone to Machu Picchu and Cuzco in Peru and then to Portillo in Chile and Temuco to ski the Volcano Llaima.

The very next year my father was too terribly busy and consumed a lot of Bourbon Whiskey so me and Graham, we were the stars of Frank's winning team and Graham was awarded the Batting Title. I had a fit as I calculated I had beaten him for the title by one point. I think we shared the crown eventually it was just politics as usual that I had been overlooked.

"I don't want you to play baseball." Said my father Louis. Dead silence.

"I have more important things for you to do." he

added but then he never explained. He never explained that he was jealous that his own son was turning out to resemble more the man in the kitchen than himself. Finally he thought that maybe I could learn to be a baker or a cook: that the servants might be able to train me. Well that never quite happened as now I only dreamed of doing sports. I found my father's old tennis racquet and hit a tennis ball against the overhead garage door until finally my father noticed it needed paint and then forbade me to play tennis there.

I was to be shipped away to boarding school in New Hampshire. The Groves were going to England again and their services wouldn't be needed anymore. My father had found a new fiance but she didn't take kindly to me even though she had two older boys of her own. The car was packed and Frank would be driving me away to my new home at Holderness School in the White Mountains of New Hampshire. Other than one half hour conversation nine years later this would be the last time I would see Caroline and Frank. I waved goodbye to Graham. T was thirteen years old now and doing what my father had done when a young boy himself. His mother had shipped him off to Fessenton, Choate and Hotchkiss, Then he had gone to Yale, an Ivy League College.

Frank was very polite and began to talk to me on the long six hour drive from Connecticut up into the wilds of New England. It was Labor Day and a few leaves were already turning yellow in the picturesque quaint little New England Villages. I liked seeing each and every one as I had been here many times with my own father Louis on ski trips to ski or visit my maternal grandparents south of Boston. Frank was almost apologetic as he sensed this would be very hard for me to suddenly move away at such a young age. I was not in his mind mature enough to weather such a change of weather. He was trying to console me that it would not be so bad as I would ski in winter and yes they would have baseball and football teams. I would be a star as he had coached me well. He knew that much and then when I finally got out of the car and my belongings were all in my room he gave me a hug goodbye which he had never done once. He began to cry as I did also. I was terrified. I missed my field mice. I missed Caroline. I missed Graham. They were my family. I would not be seeing them anymore. I felt abandoned and deserted. Frank drove away. I followed the car with my eyes until I could no longer see it.

I was traumatized by my new surroundings. My roomate was from Pakistan and a devout Muslim. He rolled out a carpet in our room between the beds and prayed when the sun went down;and prayed again when the sun came up although I could not see it as our room faced north.

"What are you doing?" I inquired'

The quarterback of my football team would become a General in the Vietnam Conflict and disobey orders to attack Laos, refusing to launch a full scale invasion. My muslim roomate I would teach to box and he would become a Navy pilot on an Aircraft Carrier and shoot down alot of Migs plus drop napalm which bothered him to his dying day because he was a devoted Muslim and knew violence begets more violence. I went out for passes as an end and caught them. Our baseball team was a disaster not worth mentioning except I was the shortstop and the only one who had been trained in the sport. Of course I made the ski team too and was happy as a clam to see so much snow and coach my young teammates, but I was having a few problems with authority. There was no psychiatrist at the school, only a nurse who kept me from dying of dehydration when I had gone with the school and made fifteen runs at Tuckerman's Ravine in one day. It literally almost killed me as I had forgotten to drink water. That same nurse within a year went through a red light in the town in thick fog and was killed by the Snowplow.

I have nothing nice to say about the headmaster of that school when I attended. His name was Hagerman and he had a beef to chew with all skiers.

"There is so much more to life than skiing. You will need a job to get married and raise a family. Then there;s college to think about and the military. I would hear none of it. Ski. Ski Ski Ski free or die! The state motto, not really. Just a joke

Daddy's gone away

Daddy you left before I could say goodbye

Daddy's gone away. Should I cry?

I will miss the very grande Norwegian Maple we planted when I was four

I will miss the very large New England Colonial with its leaky roof where I was a child

I will miss the hurricane of 1953 when we cooked everything in the fireplace and ate by candlelight

I will miss the rain that somehow leaked onto my face in spite of the brand new shingles

I will miss high flies in the backyard

I will miss running back into the stone wall and banging my head to catch that deep fly ball you hit

I will miss going to the cemetery to pay respect to your friend who died from the war

I will miss the tall spruce trees I climbed to see the schooners in Long Island Sound

I will miss the bumpy cobblestone street we lived on and the ride from the train station to pick you up

I will miss Palmer's Market where my mother took me grocery shopping to meet the policeman and the grocery clerk and his sons with girlfriends

I will miss Christmas in New York at your brother's house on Park Avenue with all the holiday lights gleaming in fresh snow

I will miss going with you to Yale Bowl to route for your college team that lost and the long drive home in the dark

I will miss the ski trips way up to Vermont at Mount Snow with your lady friend Mrs Goodyear and all her children almost my age

We stopped for Swedish Smorgasbord and you always grumbled about the bill but gladly paid it somehow

I will miss the long plane rides to Panama and Lima and Santiago over snow capped mountains, the Andes

I remember telling you that I would like to live down there

Your reply to me was that I would die, for instance, cougars would have me for dinner

I will miss our few days we skied together in Portillo and I will miss my youth

I will grow old now to be like you and have grandchildren on my knee like you

I will miss my mother who died young. I will miss the runaway dog you let me keep for a friend because I was alone

When you went on long trips all over the world I could not always come along but attended grade school at New Canaan Country Day

I will miss having a second home to go to beside my own, Grandpa's big log cabin with servants and a lanky cigar smoking chauffeur who waxed his car and put gas in it;vand all the cheerful kitchen help dressed in rags who had survived Auschwitz death camp

I will miss your sister my Aunt Fran who was always polite and considerate who goaded you over everything like a big sister should

I will miss the horses my cousins rode and all the poop in their stalls I volunteered to shovel

I will miss the chickens that ran into the raspberry and blueberry patches and the hunting dogs that were turned loose to chase the foxes

How we ran behind on foot but not having horses ourselves we missed all the action

So you took me to the car race but a tire came off one car and killed a spectator so we left hurriedly

I will miss that we grew apart when I went off to

boarding school but that I loved growing up as it was much more exciting and the world would be mine for awhile at least

I will miss that success in this world, at least for me did not last.

I will not miss being sick in midlife crisis with thyroid failure

I will not miss that you disapproved of my divorce even though she filed it against me but told my own children I had deserted them all

I will miss that you forgave me and invited me back into the family on my sixtieth birthday

There I stood at your door ringing the bell as the wet snow soaked my shoes and socks with holes

Then also like you I will not miss this life on Earth entirely because we both know now how terribly disappointing it was

You raced our speed boat out onto Long Island Sound bouncing over the waves like some young naval cadet (plebe) from Annapolis

Because that is what you always were at heart, sailing off into the high seas of adventure

So I reckon that is where you are now on some new voyage beyond the stars

I am a cadet (plebe) too. I followed in your footsteps. I sailed the high seas too

And I will follow you to the stars, Dad. Because you taught me too just as your own dad taught you

My son has come back into my life now here at your funeral he finally approaches me

Now he knows what I know what you knew and Grandpa before you…

I will miss even my cousins who began to hate and tease me, I will forgive them

Just as you have forgiven me, Father

Arlene

My birth mother had been Arlene Anderson Perry. She had been married to my birth father in Alabama after the second World War which had defeated those maniachel Germans, Japanese and Italians. She had been held captive at home there in Alabama where women were not yet liberated against her liberal Massachusetts will and had managed to escape on the bus back to her aunt Doris in Easton, Massachusetts very close to Brockton. Aunt Doris had just married a Chase for mostly good name and financial security, and she suggested to Arlene that she better find a career and give up on the idea of raising a child without a husband to support her.

So my mother gave me up for adoption for ten thousand dollars to a nice well to do couple in Weymouth, the husband of which was a Lieutenant in the U.S. Navy. And Arlene signed up with the Woman's Air Force(WAF)and served in the Korean War in Japan shortly thereafter. She was basically a cocktail waitress in an Officers Lounge and met some high brass. This landed her a job as a receptionist for Sikorsky helicopters in the mid 1950's shortly thereafter where she met an interesting fellow with a German accent, Mr. Baxter from Argentina. He had a wife probably somewhere and some daughters and a niece or some such from his relatives in California named Hodie. Possibly Hodie Hazard??? Obviously they were all Germans displaced by the War. Mr Hazard seemed attractive enough but was sort of crazy. It turned out a nice Jewish man named Kissinger had recruited him to fly as a spy for us in the Korean war and he had been shot down and wounded in the head and had a plate there on the side of his skull. He had some behavior problems and had been in an Irish Pub in New York City where he was mistaken after several beers of being a former Nazi officer so they beat him up severely and broke his one good leg, the other leg being a pegleg because it had been amputated in perhaps December 1944 in a bombing raid over Germany but then this turned out to be incorrect as he later admitted flying a plane in the Luftwaffe that was shot down by Russian ground forces near Berlin. And he just so happened to know the man who had adopted her son, me. Small world!

Arlene was of course a blonde which had attracted the German pilot, now some sort of technical advisor working for Sikorsky. Her paternal grandparents had emigrated from Motala, Sweden in the latter eighteen hundreds and been recruited brought to America in part by Ames Shovel Company of Easton, Massachusetts which explains at least in part how her family ended up there, the Andersons who I later in life hunted down to get their story but by that time of course Arlene was deceased as she had gotten that awful cancer and died in 1983 at age fifty four down where she had moved to work in a hospital in Providence, Rhode Island.

Tony Reynolds, the Monster, and my mother Thais, my Savior

I cannot remember being adopted as I was very young but I do remember the house on Cape Cod where we lived when I was three years Old.

There was sand everywhere and the lawn was very small and there were almost no trees. My father worked as a weatherman for some local radio station probably as there were still no televisions. His salary was thirty eight dollars per week which is less than a dollar per Hour, Of course gas was then nineteen cents a gallon and a hamburger about the same. A hotdog was probably ten cents with fixings.

So my father's family told him to return to nearer New York if he wanted to still be included in the family so he went shopping for a house north of Darien and found a run down New England colonial with two acres which could be purchased for twenty thousand dollars which back then was a very large sum and he borrowed it from Papa Joe his dad and he bought the overpriced house and we all moved into it. There was a runaway dog which came with the property and we adopted him eventually and I named him Rudolf after yes the famous reindeer. There were goldfish in a bowl on the porch and there were chickens in a chicken coup. There were a lot of raspberries all very thorny. My mother wanted to plant a garden and have a farm with a horse or two but my father wasn't terribly interested in spending money when we owed many thousands still to Papa Joe.

So at kindergarten my first day a very large monster of a child in my class named Tony Reynolds kept stealing all my blocks and toys. Very frustrating it was having my new environment ruined. My mother sensed my anxiety and I confessed to her everything'

So she explained to me that my ancestor was Ghenghis Khan who conquered the world on horseback and that American Indians were all related to him and that I must fight. She proceeded to teach me how to box there in the middle of our one acre back lawn.

At school Tony Reynolds at first opportunity stole everything of mine. Luckily I had good coaching as my mother had said,

"Go find the biggest block and then...

"So I found a three foot two by four and returned to near Tony Reynolds who said,

"What are you going to do?"

I knew exactly what to do. I swung that thing and knocked him right off his feet and he turned beet red after he got up and stood over a foot taller than me.

So I ran out the door and up the long leaning tree which had been knocked almost flat by the hurricane of 1953, I was way up there maybe fifteen feet off the ground and I had no plans on coming down.

The school called the police and fire department and my mother who finally was located somewhere off shopping. Her voice was soothing and reassuring and she had a great big smile. She was almost laughing with amusement:she was so proud for me taking on that class bully.

She was my hero and I became hers too.

Unfortunately less than two years later she had a mental breakdown and was taken off to a Hospital Sanatorium in Great Barrington, Massachusetts and I briefly saw her once there for twenty minutes then visited her seventeen years later for four days in Florida where she had married a realtor named Baker and they lived in a hundred thousand dollar three thousand square foot home. She died there in Florida with ten dogs who she put to sleep before her final trip to the hospital with cancer. She called me on the telephone,

"Come and see me! "I didn't get too as my wife and we were poor with children at home and arguing over money etc

Louis My Father

At the tender age of five my parents sLouis and Thais informed me that I had been adopted and that they weren't my original parents whereupon I began calling them by their first names.

For a woman my black haired Thais was a real monster. Luckily she had a sweet disposition half of the time but the other half of the time when I refused to eat my burnt overly cooked lamb chops, she spanked me and tossed me back into my crib. So I too was a little monster in her image.

My father came home every evening from New York on the train (which I had yet to discover)and appeared at the back door which she sometimes locked as her lesbian friends were retreating out of the living room by way of the front door.

Then one day an ambulance came and they carried my mother out the front door screaming. She didn't want to go to that Sanatorium in Stockbridge, Massachusetts.

My father looked at me with terror in his eyes and proclaimed,

"Now you'll do what I tell you to do!" Hardly.

So he took me with him to Washington D.C. where he applied for some government job in a very big building. I had to wait in a room somewhere until he returnedChild abuse:they didn't have a name for it back then. You did what you were told or got beat up. In Sweden they were trying something new and experimental called child psychology but in America well here we did everything with B-52s dropped bombs on them all if they wouldn't agree with us. Yes and if they might persist there was the Atomic Bomb. BANG!

On a casual drive through Jefferson, New Hampshire en route to see my grandmother Darthea in Mooselookmeguntic, Maine my father had to inspect a hotel that had been burned down by Sugar Hill resident Joseph Kiernan of the Boston Common Garage embezzlement scandal for the insurance money. My father wasn't very thorough because he explained to me that he didn't want that job with the FBI they wanted to transfer him to.

He had a job with some other Department of government. I was very little still and didn't quite understand. We would go to Lexington, Kentucky to meet his boss and then to Germany France Switzerland Italy Spain:all part of his job. I never saw him work although he attended meetings. He had been a second Lieutenant in World War Two which he had fought in Algeria in a Weather Station making forecasts for the Invasion of Sicily etc and I was later to understand from my history books that that was a very big World War which we had won so I should be very proud of my father.

But deep down inside I was already a communist although not a registered communist. My father keep talking to our ski instructor Miki Hutter from Austria about Skorzeny's military exploits rescuing Mussolini etc but on television I saw Germans in uniforms and they were all the bad guys I thought, especially the Japanese. We were taught racism in school-to hate our enemies.

But in church we were taught to love our enemies. I had gone to a Danny Kaye movie with my mother before they carted, Frank was an avid her off. Wonderful, wonderful Copenhagen the movie showed how wonderful the Danish children were: I wanted to go there. My mother said they wouldn't like me there because my father was Jewish. It was a truly confusing world, especially for a little monster in the making.

But now my mother was gone and in her place there was a whole family of house servants, the Groves from London. Evidently my father sensing that since I was of English mostly extraction this stable family would be a good influence on me and he was right because Mr Groves was an avid athlete gardner roofer soccer player and he soon coached the Masonic little league team starring his son Graham and me, while Mrs Groves, Caroline baked chocolate cakes and cleaned our house.

I took Graham on a ski adventure when it snowed. We went to the Country Club Golf course hill where he skied over a sand trap unable to turn and crashed head first yes blood and his mother wasn't too impressed grounding him.

I was eventually shipped off to a prep school in New Hampshire at age thirteen because I was continually fighting at school. That's when my father met a divorcee named Dorothy the Witch I thought. She was after his money but of course he didn't ever have any until his

DUNCAN CULLMAN

father's will was settled and then every bitch in hell was turned loose and they all had a lot of makeup and ruby red lips and a lot of hair like my mother but they shaved it and wore excessive perfume. Disgusting to a thirteen year old'

Then I turned fourteen and it somehow all made sense. The Groves all became history for me as they moved to Narragansett, Rhode Island near the beach somewhere.

I went to Chile with my father where he met some tall bald man with a German accent near Llaima Volcano we all skied but the lodge was very smokey and I got the flu while the adults climbed the volcano. The tall German looked a lot like our distant neighbor from Pound Ridge, New York who had beautiful blond daughters and golden retrievers. His wife, bald man invited me to come ski race in Argentina which was very orderly and so against my father's wishes I had boarded a train for southern Chile to join up with the Chilean ski team all young boys and girls with their chaperone Mrs Leatherby. the wife of the owner of farellones Ski Area, Chile's very first. She had been a ladies golf champion of Chile under her maiden name Gazitua.

Over in Argentina I was to stay at the very friendly but not really very friendly at all Syrian Auchless or something Refugio for Refugees of the War(they lost) and an Israeli showed up with a gun. I had met him evidently in Portillo, Chile. Now I wanted to forget him:but the gun was loaded and cocked.

"Okay you can spend the night" I agreed.

My fathers friend Doctor Little in Bozeman, Montana sent a kindly telegram which stated,

"YOU HAVE BEEN KIDNAPPED>LEAVE AT ONCE>GET ON THE FIRST TRAIN TO BUENOS AIRES. TELL THEM YOU HAVE A FAMILY EMERGENCY YOU MUST LEAVE>OR TELL THEM NOTHING AT ALL JUST GO GET OUT OF THERE!"

Dear Louis, I'm having a good time here in Argentina there is more snow than New Hampshire and the mountains are bigger, I may never come home at all, well when I run out of money but it's not costing me much at all. And besides I don't like stepmother all that much but I see why you do-big teats!

My grandmother Wolf was very anxious for me and hired two operatives to rescue me, all for a big sum of money of course. They were brothers of the same father and I never learned their names but realized there cover was blown and they were probably executed. Later their father put a hit on me much later.

I was young and naïve, not exactly all my fault.

my father visited Paul Valar in Sugar Hill and accused him of hiding Nazis even though he was Swiss and his wife Paula a bronze medalist from Czechoslovakia. They had no idea my father was the U'S. Government at least not at first. The government wanted all those German patriots down in Argentina and Chile to kill communists. Our beloved government was still at war.

The Secret Life of Louis Coleman

Growing up in greater New York City I learned that delivery men were Italians, bartenders and cooks were Irish, dishwashers and field hands were blacks. Of course there were people who had shiny new cars and wore suits and ties and those were the English. My father instructed me that the English now ruled the world.

There were the French from France and they had been collaborators with Hitler and so had been expelled from the New Postwar France of Charles De Gaulle whom everyone in America detested as he wanted to withdraw France from NATO. There were French in Canada but those were mostly Indians descended from trappers who took natives for wives as no Parisian beauties could be found to freeze their delicate French asses in North America.

We lived in Fairfield County in Connecticut, a New England State that had originally been settled by the Dutch so it really was more like New York than Massachusetts.

My mother Thais was originally from Boston where she rode horses as a young girl with her sister Jean and brother Ned behind their house in Hingham in a large apple orchard. I was very fortunate to be adopted by rich people and live in the richest nation on Earth, the United States of America which had just won two World Wars : and dropped the Atomic Bomb on Japan, game over.

Now there was lasting world peace in the New Order with the American President telling everyone in the world by radio and television (a new invention) just what that would be.

My father was a little bit different as he was Jewish and Hitler had just killed six million of his kinds. Apparently nobody liked them as they had too much money. My mother didn't seem to mind as she went shopping for groceries and the latest gossip.

Albeit about my father being different, he was white like his older sister Nan whose real name was Francis. When he was born his mother, my granny Wolfe, told him,

"I didn't want you!" He was born last of five siblings and she had apparently already had it, meaning she was fed up with everything from breast feeding to babies crying in the middle of every night every year for twelve in a row.

My father's poor luck to be the very last and unwanted. Even his own brothers didn't want him. Somebody started a rumor that my granny Wolfe was having an extra marital affair with some German who probably raped her in a taxi cab or limousine off in some forest who knows where.

So my father attended Choate, Hotchkiss and Yale in that order, having been sent away to boarding school at age twelve because of my granny Wolfe's guilty conscience or just because she was a lazy bitch or that's what my grandfather Joseph called her.

Joseph Coleman III was the son of Joseph Coleman Jr who my father never spoke much about as probably nobody liked him. The Coleman men were very tough on their women and children, scolding them constantly like Londoners. They had come to Cologne, Germany via London where one had managed to marry the red haired granddaughter of the Bishop of Cambridge, John Hall.

Some Colemans had arrived on Ellis Island, New York as immigrants in the late nineteenth century and soon found work delivering newspapers on bicycles. They worked their way up to eventually become Coleman Bros., a respectable New York Firm including Philip Morris Tobacco, Benson and Hedges Tobacco Company and Marlboro Cigarettes. Joseph Coleman III was very enhanced marrying Francis Wolfe whose Dutch Indies family had relocated in Dutch Guyiana and actually knew the tobacco industry inside out.

My father's two older brothers Joseph IV and Edgar planned on cutting him out of the family business from day one B.C. before time even was invented. His brother Arthur managed to escape the family with a teaching degree and became the Dean of Ohio University.

My father actually thought he might be German as opposed to a Jew whose ancestors lived in Germany. Charles Lindberg flew a plane across the Atlantic Ocean and he was a sympathizer with Hitler. Germany was on the move ideologically and in mass production.

Furthermore, the German people were the Master Race. So was my father also from about six years old onward.

So at Yale he joined the Bundes League of German Brethren who all drank beer and went skiing and sang German songs, although my father rarely sang because his voice was nasty.

Possibly at Yale his infiltration of the Bundesliga made him an attractive candidate for the U.S. Government which wanted to know who were these sympathizers with Adolf Hitler.

I only know there was a Bundes Book and a Browning automatic in the little drawer in the bed stand. I never asked him about it after mentioning it once as he said to me,

"You didn't see it!"

There was one particular acquaintance of my father, a tall man mostly bald with a few locks of blond hair and very bad breath who apparently had no name. I was told that I never had met him and not to mention him to anyone. He was at Yale Bowl in the restroom coming up behind my father at the urinal. He was a cruel man with a very mean and bitter attitude because Germany had lost the war. We met him at some other person's house where I was told to go play in the yard. We met him again at llaima Volcano in Chile where he and my father talked extensively. I met him without my father on the chairlift at Alpine Meadows during the Junior National Ski Competition. He coached me well that day in spite of his cynical bad attitude on life in general. He told me to just ski down the course and make it to the finish line as most of the young ski racers would not as it was a blizzard. i finished sixth but won the next year at Bend, Oregon. I had finally escaped both my father and that strange man

Eight Years Old and the Ark

I was still a child and eight years old when my father and I were invited by my uncles and cousins to go to a Hebrew Synagogue on the upper west side of New York not to far north of Central Park but northerly enough to be influenced by Haarlem which had become an African-American neighborhood. We took a taxi there. I remember it as being early autumn.

I considered myself a baseball player at the time with a bright future in Little League. We had great coaches with moral values. I played for the catholic team the Knights of Columbus but in a few years I would change to the Kiwanis team sponsored by the Masons, I cannot remember exactly as I was more interested in the game of baseball, Mickey Mantle, Yogi Berra and Roger Maris of the New York Yankees.

So we all crowded into this apartment and over by the piano, well it looked like a piano but it was golden, a big mysterious looking thing. I have never seen anything like that ever since or before.

Don t look at it my father warned me

So we went to our seats and someone turned out the lights. And my cousins who were devoted Hebrews warned me not to open my eyes because God was going to come out of that contraption and would kill us if we dared to open our eyes.

And someone said that maybe it wasn't working at all.

And someone else said to be quiet God was just not yet sure about us that we had to be more sincere

We waited. If God was coming out of that box there was no way I was going to miss the show and suddenly as I opened my eyes a light came crawling out of the box and saw my open eyes uh-oh.

I passed out cold.

There were creatures of all shapes and sizes of all creations in all planets all seraphim and I was totally afraid like never in my entire life and then came some cherubim and perhaps some angels.

I lay on the floor when the lights came back on in the room but I was still unconscious there surrounded by my unbelieving cousins including Susan who said something to the effect that I must have opened my eyes and was indeed dead

Suddenly I woke up from my spell and I had not seen God but had seen too much and had been terribly afraid but now I was overjoyed to see my cousins laughing at me.

Ana, La Santa

Dear Ana,

Your cousin the cook was outside your restaurant on the sidewalk shaking her ass in a flowery mini-skirt trying to attract Colombian passerbys into your Mexican restaurant at a time when Mexican drug wars were headline news, bodies in piles.

She definitely caught my attention her wild brown playful eyes and the attention of a young couple so we entered and ordered the big burrito.

Then you showed up from the bank where your loan officer was nervous.

Then your daughter and son both appeared from school somewhere nearby there in Normandie, a barrio in greater Bogota home of eight million people spread out quite distantly so there are a lot of parks and trees everywhere in the Anti-plano, a high mountain valley between ridges of twelve thousand foot forested peaks the city lies at about nine thousand feet.

Your son realizing you were talking to a North American tourist wanted to ask me if I liked football(as that is what they call soccer)and I replied,

"Yes, Messi the Argentine is very good and diego Forlan, the Uruguayan. Neymar and Ronaldino the Brazilians are also very good."

Your daughter wanted to know where I came from and I responded,

"Boston, Massachusetts in Estados Unidos but north in the countryside near the border with Canada."

She didn't know where that was exactly but it satisfied her curiosity for the moment to know such a place might exist but it was so far distant that I might as well have come from the moon itself.

In Colombia they are quite swarthy men much more so than Peru which is more indian Quechua, Inca, Moche!

I, not being swarthy and not dressed in a dinner jacket and tie with pointed alligator shoes didn't quite fit her equation of Colombian normalcy.

Both your children are well dressed and smart as whips which is what you had wanted for yourself as well as you were born up farther north in a similar mountain valley no North Americans have ever visited overnight and it's not in our atlas map of Colombia:there are thousands of such villages in Colombia not so in Peru which is overrun by New Yorkers as well as everyone else even Europeans.

In Colombia the American tourists are mostly in the larger cities near police or with guides not venturing too far into the unknown which is everywhere Colombian except for the Colombians themselves descended from the Spanish Conquistadors twenty generations ago so they each and everyone knows every square inch at least where their ancestors had trod.

Every time I come to Colombia thereafter I keep visiting you and your growing children who are yes bigger and taller, more grown up now they are ready to attend the university.

While you, although separated for ten years, refuse to file for a divorce as it would be too expensive and you insist you can't go through it all a second time your nerves worn a little thin perhaps.

Colombia is a Catholic country and the ant-iplano is very conservative, not like the coastal regions more known for salsa and African drums. So divorce is easier with a pistol or arsenic or by running away to Bolivia or Ecuador but that is not so easy either.

We have all been caught up in the trap of who we have become all these formative years into later adulthood so we are afraid to venture into the unknown like a gringo tourist in a remote Colombian jungle.

But this is true for the mass of humanity, aging brings on conservatism.

So the years pass by and I am on my computer surfing the web for yet another cheap ticket to Bogota or Asuncion with a stop in Bogota, or for a ticket from Bogota to the Andes where I can ski for a week.

I drive my car every morning to the same breakfast Café to be served by the same smiling waitress wondering where I am going this year to escape!

Every night all summer long I drive to the same softball field and see my teammates who ask me if I'm going on another South American adventure.

"Well", I answer," The local women want nothing to do with me and I don't indulge with prostitutes anywhere, the foreign women are much more interesting and they think I am perhaps from Mars.

I try not to disappoint them. I tell them all about baseball which they have only seen on television but never played.

and the vast majority of South Americans have never skied except for a few rich :though some have gone to the Andes and made snowballs after riding a chairlift in rented ski parkas and snow pants and snow boots.

The time goes by, the minutes into hours and weeks into years, and I see a message from Ana on facebook from Ana.

"Is it true that you are coming to Bogota next month? It will be so good to see you! We can go to coffee someplace nearby.

The children will want to see you but they have children of their own who have heard you are from Mars and will land in your spaceship near the Airport.

O children always love a good story, the world has not changed one iota and neither has ana!

Earthling, Mother of God, Blessed Virgin daughter of God and kindness and all that is best and good, sweet Ana.

We Follow Jesus in our procesion

We follow Jesus in our procession

We follow Jesus with His cross

On foot on bicycle on skates on horse(but not in cars alone)

Through clouds of smog and doubt

Because His Words of Faith are the Way are the Path

We had lost our faith we had lost our way and stumbled

Our bride had been taken from us

We were robbed by false doctrines, by false practitioners

Who took our money but could not cure us

There is only One Healer, One Doctor for our ills

He is followed by one thousand umbrellas in a tearful procession

Through raindrops of our weeping

About the destruction of our environment

Our mother the planet

"Come back to your mother you lost people!"

We were conquered and sent it the captivity of despair

For our sins but we now repent

Of our lust and greed, we had lost our way in darkness

But now our Nation shall be restored to us

He will place us once again on our Holy Hill Jerusalem
in Zion

Because hope is now lifted up within us

"Go and sin no more, pollute no more nor sit in laziness"

"But rise up and breath and Walk as He does!"

Now the sunshine shall be returned to us

Let us be jubilant and joyous

Now that Eden is restored, Our Garden Eternal!

We had families before but now we have only Jesus
Our Saviour

I have seen Him, He is Risen

He is there in Chia we have seen him

He is there and everywhere

Now He liberates our conquered City

Now he sets us captives free

Find Him and Live forevermore!

Gina,

My love

In the morning you are here to great my new day

Like the sun warming my every shivering appendage

Like a kiss to connect me to the memory of my mother

Who first brought me into this world

To know of your love.

Father, I learned to love you too from your love

You were there to keep all our love from spoiling into passion and temper

You were like the cold blue sky

Ever constant ever deep like eternity

This eternal love because our mother earth keeps on spinning

Round and round like your arms wrapped all around me and your legs

To support the foundation of us we are family

Even dogs and cats with our many babies

Fish and flying things, birds singing in the trees now
sprouting

Light green budding like our love.

When I first saw your face

We were both married to other unfaithfuls

Never imagining that one day we might yet discover
in each other

True and lasting love, it is like a songbird singing

Or like a soft warm breeze,

And so I kissed you or

No, you kissed me.

How did this happen?

From out of nowhere our grand collision in space,

We were just meant to be

In love

Atop whitest mountain peaks, skiing, snowboarding
and snow shoeing

Singing our song and dancing our dance

Of life and love

For they are one and we

Are the inheritors of the Truth and the kingdom

Trouble Near Times' Square

"You can help us again" said my father then repeated himself,

"We can use you one more time."

Somewhere in the back of my mind I knew this meant challenging work, maybe even dangerous work but I was much too hopeful and optimistic.

"They've been following Dorothy's car" he indicated there was a problem.

"Who are they"?" I inquired.

"Arabs," is all he said, "Arabs."

"Oh, well what do I have to do?" I really didn't like my stepmother a whole lot as she had turned against me from day one but now I felt some remote sympathy for her that she was somehow in danger. I thought or was hoping it wasn't my own fault in any way but I knew probably that was. I had been drunk near Times' Square at some strip joint. She was a Greek belly dancer and I even paid money to talk to her maybe forty dollars. It turned out she was a Lebanese, not a Greek and we began talking about my family situation. I had volunteered too much information that my step-mother worked for Channel Thirteen PBS as a fundraiser and that my father who adopted me was Jewish. What had they put in my drink to make me talk so much? Was I

~ 167 ~

really that unhappy living in my father's house again at age twenty seven after I had run away more or less at age sixteen to ski with Nazis in Argentina. These were more of my father's inner circle of definitely CIA associates or was he a closet Nazi I didn't dare ask him ever.

"Drive Dorothy's car, the Mercedes to New Hampshire and "They" will be following you. Don't speed or you will lose them just drive the speed limit." I agreed to do whatever he said as this was indeed serious. I sensed I had fucked up big time.

So I pulled onto the interstate and I could see I was being tailed all the way to Boston but then I didn't see any other car on the long drive to North Conway where I parked the car near Rita Thompson's house and went to talk to her son Jimmy Thompson, my friend but he wasn't home and had gone to Taos to see his wife.

I didn't think too much of the entire episode as I had done as directed, followed my father's orders. There had been a time when as still a boy of fourteen, he had me swear an oath of allegiance to the flag. It was some procedure I had to undergo in order to take microfilm in my suitcase to Chile to the ski patrolman in Portillo named Roy Shaefer. I didn't know what microfilm was or what it contained or even where in my luggage it was hidden.

"Just deliver the entire suitcase to him" my father had instructed me.

So then I drove my stepmother's car around town showing it off proudly as none of my friends there had ever seen me driving anything quite so flashy. I was following instructions not knowing what the consequences might be. This was very long ago and before Al Qaeda was even in the news or its existence known to the American public. Probably it was known in Israel, Lebanon, Jordan and Palestine by then.

When out of my father's supervision it seemed trouble was my middle name.

Dorothy, my stepmother, knew that and told me to go hang out on the West Side near the Docks and listen for information as a fifteen year old. Maybe I was a stupid kid because I went down there like a gullable child. The first guy I met told me,

"Look kid your stepmother must want to get you killed as people down here with any information get their throats cut and sleep with the fishes." Slowly I was gaining wisdom but very slowly.

So my very Jewish stepmother now had some extra attention and my own father felt this was indeed a credible threat. Maybe he thought I was a credible threat. It would seem so as things turned out.

In North Conway there was "The man" someone told me. Someone else told me that the entire "Strip" of commercial property from one end to the other had been bought by "The mob" before World War Two so probably in the days of Prohibition (of alcohol). The gangsters back then had all the loot (money) from Speakeasies (illegal bars).

Anyway my father in his capacity as whatever his title was with the government went to visit the father of my then girlfriend Bob Fisher whose close neighbors were chemists and pharmacists. It seemed the regime of Richard Nixon was quite concerned about the Hippy

Rebellion and thought of making very strong LSD to distribute among the dissidents for free for the specific purpose of keeping them all high as a kite.

Various parents plus other local volunteers were learning the art of making very strong little pills like "Jacob's Ladder" in this laboratory on Conway Lake in that exclusive subdivision which was called South Conway but was a little farther south there in the woods and tiny fields on long dirt roads back then.

I think there were some families who didn't have sufficient funds for their children to be "U.S. Ski Team Members" or the equivalent and needed extra money to feed them all as the Vietnam War economy was beginning to impact the entire economy.

I not quite grasping all of the above but soon discovered perhaps that knowing too much indeed I had now become expendable. I was basically just a poor hippie with rich parents somewhere who it seems had no interest in supporting me. So I found sympathy from a young native American woman with a child whose young husband a welder informed me that the place he worked was "Really a front for the Mafia but don't use that word as they preferred to be called "The family". I was already learning much too much as he fixed me up with some young bar maid by Mickying her. She took me home but I wandered out to pee in the night looking for a restroom. I opened a door and flipped on a switch and lo and behold it was some kind of an LSD factory.

"You've seen too much!" she confided to me. Her parents owned Salmon Press and the Littleton Courier but they had thought it best for her that she join the underworld. So there we were suddenly cast together "In Hell" or at the very edge of it a huge precipice like Tuckerman Ravine itself

The Monastic Life at
St. Bernard's Monastery Ski Area

The Monastery St. Bernard

After exploring south and west in the land of more sun
and higher mountains I purchased for two thousand
nine hundred ninety nine dollars a patented mining
claim entitled Bastile at eleven thousand eight hundred
fifty feet altitude, roughly twice the altitude of Mt
Washington, New Hampshire;and thereupon after
selling my original one acre of land in Twin Mountain,
New Hampshire in order to complete the sale with a five
thousand mile drive in an orange Datsun hallucinating
most of the way just from exhaustion, I henceforce began
to build a monstrous ten by ten foot cabin with some
Ohio hitchikers I had picked up on the way west:most
notably Ken Saffranski who insisted on picking up his
girlfriend Dianne Stauder who was pleased with herself
to find a ride in any direction after having flunked
out of Ohio State her sophomore year due to excessive
drinking drugs and wild sex orgies. She proceeded to
be so happy she insisted on doing both of us and I being
sloppy seconds managed to bring her to an unrivaled
climax thereupon she became my girlfriend for almost
two years.

I knew Mynx might not be too thrilled about my new companion as Mynx had been up there first to the "Monastery" we called it. But Mynx was preoccupied in distant adventures with her Daddy sailing the Atlantic.

Hank Dane and later his girlfriend Michelle Spanos would come visit from Sugar Hill and Indian Head Resort in Franconia Notch. Then Safransky brought his college mate Gus Campagna who found in a bar some Nick Nohava whose last name was an alias as Indiana wanted him but he couldn't go back there! Like the song definitely.

We would drive to town, buy rice, potatoes bullets and beer more beer. The monks seemed to have a passion more for beer and less for brewing wine which was too time consuming. We were so busy playing croquet, horseshoes, skiing on summer snow and inviting every character we could find in Silverton and nationwide to come visit eleven thousand nine hundred feet overnight then climb the grassy ridge to Bonita Peak thirteen thousand two hundred feet. Mynx saved my life in a rainstorm on the far side of the mountain where we had gone on a ski adventure scantily clad in tee shirts when she produced out of a plastic mini-jar three matches of which the third was successful in starting a bonfire. But Mynx was history now. New adventurers arrived from France with indescribable expressions on their faces as they had expected a full hostel with running water.

"Oh we run on over there to the stream for our water!" explained Gus to the awestruck travelers who replied,

"This is not a hostel how did you get a license, in France it is very difficult?"

"Well we are in the process of building the hostel" I pointed to the site seventy yards distant where our fourth building was under construction.

Luckily the Frenchmen and their woman had brought some acid LSD and then there was a nonstop party into the next day so they had fun but departed and we lost our license oh well.

Nick and Gus went to work for Mrs Stone a hairdresser from Manhattan who bought a mountaintop of mining claims on the advice of her distant fortune teller who told her to dig straight down into the center of the earth and find rare gems. She had propane heat in her luxurious abode at thirteen thousand four hundred feet while Nick and Gus claimed they shivered sleeping in some kind of cave up there. The bulldozer driver lost his life maintain her road while her husband was very understanding as it was all her money anyway...

Nick and Gus came back to the Monastery after she failed to pay them, another Silverton, Colorado mining story.

So we rescued Phyllis a telephone operator in Grand Junction from her job she hated anyway. She was struggling with her tendency toward alcoholism but at the Monastery alcohol was the alleviant to boredom so she fell off the wagon then moved into town with an Indian selling turquoise then joined a religious cult found God and moved to Texas.

So Nick and Gus went with my good friend from North Conway Jimmy Thompson to Taos where they learned the Hemp farming business and soon produced a few tons for distribution. Thereupon Gus remembered his religious commitments to the Monastery and envisioned God Jesus who told him to throw his portion of the righteous weed into the Rio Grande River which He did and so was saved. Of course Nick flipped out grabbed what he could and departed for the drug trade never to be seen again except perhaps by Jesus Himself perhaps at the Gate.

Dianne too found a higher calling and flew away on a jet plane to Ireland where she fell in love married had two children and proceeded to love mostly "Men of the Sea". At least Gus is my distant friend on facebook to this day and he is in contact with her and her sister who after using my ski poles left them at the ski area. Jimmy Thompson told me all his war stories so I wrote them down, his hiding under a blasted tree as his position was overrun by North Vietnamese Regulars. He had smoked a lot of the righteous weed and was suffering some paranoia with his post traumatic stress. Poor baby. Yes we all are poor babies way down deep inside like Led Zeppelin the song.

The Monastery was sold to an aspiring monk from Telluride for fifteen thousand dollars as unfortunately we had all grown up and moved elsewhere. Jesus, I am sure, follows us everywhere still I hope-

Flying

I had the not so enjoyable but somewhat thrilling plane ride while still handcuffed I was begging for them to be removed as I was lowered into my seat in the German Air Force Trainer plane its propeller now loudly turning over it made a hell of a lot of noise then taxied into position and took off. I was still under the influence of sodium pentathol or some other drugs prescribed to me by the man with the mustache, Dr Fritz who had been in the ski troops he claimed at or near Stalingrad. I must have passed out with my eyes rolling back in my head until of course the plane rolled sharply very sharply now we were upside down and that's when I proceeded to vomit all over the canopy above me but now it was below me the plane going into a dive I lost my stomach, so to speak. Of course I hadn't eaten in three days, perhaps a few glasses of water and a few tablespoons of soup probably with drugs in it and those shots they kept giving me probably to keep me sedated.

The plane had some kind of whistle but not quite as loud as a Stuka dive bomber as the Argentines had complained that it startled their cattle chickens livestock and made to many children cry so Rudel was prohibited from dive bombing over the downtown Bariloche as he had once or twice when drunk. He liked to drink but the plate in his head required other drugs prescribed by Mengel some doctor, I didn't quite get the name. Anyway the consumption of alcohol was not recommended and in fact warned against as it might produce some psychological problems such as pronounced repeated hysterical laughter while dive bombing, kidnapping or murdering all of these apparently his specialties. I was a mere sixteen years of age and despite their protests especially Otto with the scar, the big man who was terribly mean and kept slapping me-I kept passing out going unconscious.

"The problem with torturing children," said otto Skorzeny, "Is that they keep passing out, robbing us of all our pleasure!"

I didn't know if all their pleasure would ever cease at all but then a detective and Mrs Leatherby, the Chilean Ski Team chaperone found me in some motel room where I had been deposited and the detective made my drink nonstop coffee to bring me out of me coma as permanent brain damage had been their objective for me the suspect spy.

Mrs Leatherby came up with her best plan for my getaway by placing a scarf on my head a ribbon bangs and lipstick and yes a dress I was wearing as we were loaded into the boat to cross the big lake to go back to Chile, An old Constable and thirty young boys dressed in Lederhosen and Bavarian attire then approached the dock, "Vee are looking for that American did you see him? We are too arrest him!" They were looking and I was acting like a poor peasant mapuche maid with my shoulders slumped yes we were soon lakebound despite all their protesting the boat captain insisted he had a schedule to keep. I left Argentina. But in Chile Mrs Leatherby had a marine stand guard to my room in Puerto Varas then in Santiago she said I must go to Portillo on my own so I took a bus to Los Andes where I met my friends the Syrian Arab family who had heard the rumor some strange men were looking for me and it was Sunday with no train going to Portillo so they recommended I go with their sons up to the Christ statue about a three mile walk uphill as no Nazis would go there. I did. Next day I went to Portillo where ski patrol Schafer was furious and said my father had just arrived by plane and was coming to get me take me home. I had disobeyed orders, I would be courtmarshaled and stripped of rank, discharged from the Navy

Skiing near Llaima Volcano in Chile with Rudel

In 1960 at age twelve I had the very good fortune to accompany my father and his new lady friend, Anne Wing, to Chile in South America. We skied Portillo for over a week and then headed south by DC-3, a two engine propeller plane which was made popular by WWII to Temuco where it never stopped raining. There were many indigenous Chilean natives who were seemingly everywhere. The tall blond man who looked much too familiar hated these dark skinned people considering them to be an infernal race of imbeciles.

Where had he come from and why did he harbor so much resentment? Being a child I could not quite understand such an attitude. Yet in grade school I had already been taught that the Catholic Church had kept humanity in the Dark Ages until the Renaissance when science was born.

The ski lodge was very dirty and smoke filled the entire building whenever the wind blew which was constantly. I coughed a lot and detested this inferior ski area. It was nothing compared to Portillo but evidently the blond man had invited us to Southern Chile to see his homeland. He looked like someone I had seen before, another one of my father's strange acquaintances in New

Canaan, Connecticut but this was thousands of miles away on a different continent altogether.

When I asked my father about this strange man he said,

"You never saw him. This is a secret meeting for our government. Remember nothing about this man. Forget you ever saw him."

We then traveled to Peru and visited Machu Picchu which was a jungle snake infested "Shangri La "for the Inca Empire.

Maybe at some point Anne Wing left us as she was no longer needed to make us appear to be a normal tourist family. Just my father and I went to the Monastery above Cuzco where my father knocked loudly on the door. finally a man answered and summoned the Bishop who informed my father that the person of interest no longer resided there and had gone to Bolivia and maybe Paraguay.

This person of interest was Martin Bormann, Hitler's Personal Assistant. Had he been hiding in the Abby dressed up perhaps as a friar?

We then flew home as my father was to meet some very important people somewhere. None of my business all this I had to return to grade school at New Canaan Country Day School where I would fight Clausen daily over our common girlfriend Kathy Graham who doted on all our attention.

João Goulart

From Wikipedia, the free encyclopedia

Jump to navigation Jump to search

This name uses Portuguese naming customs: the first or maternal family name is *Marques* and the second or paternal family name is *Goulart*.

This article **needs additional citations for verification**. Please help improve this article by adding citations to reliable sources. Unsourced material may be challenged and removed.

Find sources: "João Goulart" – news · newspapers · books · scholar · JSTOR *(September 2013) (Learn how and when to remove this template message)*

His Excellency

João Goulart
President of Brazil**In office**
8 September 1961 – 1 April 1964Prime Minister

- Tancredo Neves
- Brochado da Rocha
- Hermes Lima

Preceded byRanieri Mazzilli (acting)Succeeded byRanieri Mazzilli (acting) Vice President of Brazil **In office**

31 January 1956 – 7 September 1961President

- Juscelino Kubitschek
- Jânio Quadros

Preceded byCafé FilhoSucceeded byJosé Maria AlkminMinister of Labour, Industry and Trade**In office**

18 June 1953 – 23 February 1954PresidentGetúlio VargasPreceded byJosé de Segadas VianaSucceeded

byHugo de Araújo FariaFederal Deputy from Rio Grande do SulIn office

1 February 1951 – 1 February 1955

Leave of absence: 1951–52, 1953–54State Deputy of Rio Grande do SulIn office

31 January 1947 – 31 January 1951Personal detailsBornJoão Belchior Marques Goulart

1 March 1918

São Borja, Rio Grande do Sul, BrazilDied6 December 1976 (aged 58)

Mercedes, Corrientes, ArgentinaCause of death

- Heart attack (official)[2]
- Poisoning (theorized)[3]

Resting placeCemitério Jardim da Paz

São Borja, Rio Grande do Sul, Brazil[1]Political partyPTB (1946–1966)Spouse(s)Maria Teresa Fontela (m. 1955; his death 1976) ChildrenJoão Vicente Goulart (b. 1956)

Denise Goulart (b. 1957)ParentsVicente Rodrigues Goulart

Vicentina Marques Goulart Signature

João Belchior Marques Goulart (gaúcho Portuguese pronunciation: [ʒuˈẽw bew.kiˈɔr ˈmarkis ɡuˈlar], or [ˈʒwẽw bewˈkjɔʁ ˈmaʁkiʒ ɡuˈlaʁ] in the standard Fluminense dialect; 1 March 1918 – 6 December 1976) was a Brazilian politician who served as the 24ᵗʰ president of Brazil until a military coup d'état deposed him on 1 April 1964. He was considered the last left-wing president of Brazil until Lula da Silva took office in 2003.[4]

Contents

- 1 Name
- 2 Early life
- 3 Political career
  - 3.1 Beginning at PTB
  - 3.2 Minister of Labor
  - 3.3 Vice President
- 4 The Goulart administration
  - 4.1 Basic reforms
- 5 The military coup
- 6 Life in exile
- 7 Death
- 8 Political views
  - 8.1 Afro-Brazilians
  - 8.2 Communism
- 9 Tributes and amnesty
- 10 See also
- 11 References
- 12 Sources
- 13 External links

Name

João Goulart was nicknamed **"Jango"** ([ˈʒẽgu]). The Jânio Quadros–João Goulart presidential bid was thus called "Jan–Jan" ([ʒẽ.ʒẽ], an amalgamation of Jânio and Jango).

His childhood nickname was "Janguinho" (little Jango), after an uncle named Jango. Years later, when he entered politics, he was supported and advised by Getúlio Vargas, and his friends and colleagues started to call him Jango.

His grandfather, Belchior Rodrigues Goulart, descended from Portuguese immigrants from the Azores who arrived in Rio Grande do Sul in the second half of the 18th century. There were at least three immigrants with the surname Govaert (latter adapted to Goulart or Gularte in Portuguese) of Flemish-Azorean origins in the group of first Azoreans established in the state.

Early life

Goulart was born at Yguariaçá Farm, in Itacurubi, São Borja, Rio Grande do Sul, on 1 March 1918. His parents were Vicentina Marques Goulart, a housewife, and Vicente Rodrigues Goulart, an estancieiro (a rancher who owned large rural properties) who had been a National Guard colonel fighting on the side of Governor Borges de Medeiros during the 1923 Revolution. Most sources indicate that João was born in 1918, but his birth year is actually 1919; his father ordered a second birth certificate adding a year to his son's age so that he could attend the law school at the Universidade Federal do Rio Grande do Sul.[5]

Yguariaçá Farm was isolated and his mother had no medical care at his birth, only the assistance of her mother, Maria Thomaz Vasquez Marques. According to João's sister Yolanda, "my grandmother was the one able to revive little João who, at birth, already looked like he was dying." Like most Azorean descendants, Maria Thomaz was a devout Catholic. While trying to revive her grandson, warming him, she prayed to John the Baptist, promising that if the newborn survived, he would be his namesake and would not cut his hair until the age of three, when he would march in the procession of 24 June dressed as the saint.

João grew up as a skinny boy in Yguariaçá along with his five sisters, Eufrides, Maria, Yolanda, Cila, and Neuza. Both of his younger brothers died prematurely. Rivadávia (born 1920) died six months after birth, and Ivan (born 1925), to whom he was deeply attached, died of leukemia at 33.

João left for the nearby town of Itaqui to study because his father Vicente wished to form a partnership with Protásio Vargas, Getúlio's brother, after both leased a small refrigerator house in Itaqui from an English businessman. While Vicente ran the business for the following years, João attended the School of the Teresian Sisters of Mary, along with his sisters. Although it was a mixed-sex school during the day, he could not stay overnight at the boarding school with his sisters; he had to sleep at the house of a friend of his father. It was in Itaqui that João developed a taste for both football and swimming.

Upon his return to São Borja, ending his experience as a partner in the refrigerator house, Vicente sent João to the Ginásio Santana, run by the Marist Brothers in Uruguaiana. João attended first to fourth grade in the Santana boarding school, but failed to be approved for the fifth grade in 1931. Angry with his son's poor achievements at school, Vicente sent him to attend the Colégio Anchieta in Porto Alegre. In the state capital, João lived at a pension with friends Almir Palmeiro and Abadé dos Santos Ayub, the latter of whom was very attached to him.

Aware of João's football skills at school, where he played the right-back position, Almir and Abadé convinced him to try out for Sport Club Internacional. João was selected for the club's juvenile team. In 1932, he became a juvenile state champion. That same year, he finished the third grade of the ginásio (high school) at Colégio Anchieta, with an irregular academic record that would be repeated when he attended the law school at Rio Grande do Sul Federal University. João graduated from high school at Ginásio Santana after being sent back to Uruguaiana.

Political career

Sent back to Porto Alegre after graduating from high

school, Jango attended law school to satisfy his father, who desired that he earn a degree. While there, Jango restored contact with his youth friends Abadé Ayub and Salvador Arísio, and made new friends and explored the state capital's nightlife. It was during that time of a bohemian lifestyle that Jango acquired a venereal disease,[6] which paralyzed his left knee almost entirely. His family paid for expensive medical treatment, including a trip to São Paulo, but he expected that he would never walk normally again. Because of the paralysis of his knee, Jango graduated separately from the rest of his class in 1939. He would never fully practice law.

After graduating, Jango returned to São Borja. His depression because of the leg problem was visible. He isolated himself at Yguariaçá Farm. According to his sister Yolanda, his depression did not last long. In the early 1940s, he decided to make fun of his own walking disability in the Carnival, participating in the parade of the block Comigo Ninguém Pode.

Beginning at PTB

Jango's father died in 1943, and he inherited rural properties that made him one of the most influential *estancieiros* of the region. Upon the resignation of President Getúlio Vargas and his return to São Borja in October 1945, Jango was already a wealthy man. He did not need to enter politics to rise socially, but the frequent meetings with Vargas, a close friend of his father, were decisive in Jango's pursuit of a public life.

The first invitation Jango received to enter a political party was made by Protásio Vargas, Getúlio's brother, who was in charge of organizing the Social Democratic Party (Partido Social Democrático – PSD) in São Borja. Jango declined but later accepted Getúlio's invitation to join the Brazilian Labour Party (Partido Trabalhista Brasileiro – PTB). He was the first president of the local PTB, and would later become the statewide, then national, president of the party.

In 1947, Getúlio convinced Jango to run for a seat in the state assembly. He was elected with 4,150 votes, becoming the fifth-most of 23 deputies. He received more votes than had his future brother-in-law Leonel Brizola, another rising star of the PTB, who was married to Jango's sister Neusa until her death in 1993. Jango was not an active member of the assembly but fought for the right of the needy to buy cheaper food. He soon became a confidant and political protégé of Vargas, becoming one of the party members who most insistently urged him to launch a presidential candidacy for the 1950 elections. On 19 April 1949, Jango launched Getúlio's candidacy for president at a birthday party held for the former president at Granja São Vicente, which was owned by Goulart.

In 1950, Goulart was elected to the Chamber of Deputies. He received 39,832 votes, second-most in the PTB in Rio Grande do Sul, and took office as a deputy in February 1951. He soon became secretary of the interior and a justice in the administration of Governor Ernesto Dornelles. During his time as secretary, which lasted until 24 March 1952, Jango restructured the prison system to improve the living conditions of prisoners. He later resigned his job as secretary, at the request of Vargas, to help the president with a political deadlock at the ministry of labor, using his influence on the labor-union movement.

Minister of Labor

In 1953, after becoming aggravated with the deadlock, Vargas appointed Jango minister of labor. The Vargas administration was in a deep crisis; the workers, unsatisfied with their low wages, were promoting strikes, and the right-wing party National Democratic Union (União Democrática Nacional – UDN) was mobilizing a coup d'état among the mass media, the upper-middle class, and the military forces. As he took office, Jango replied to accusations from several newspapers, including the *New York Times*. As minister of labor, Goulart held the first Brazilian Congress of Social Security. He signed a series of decrees favoring social security, such as housing financing, regulation of loans by the Institute of Retirement and Pensions of Bank Employees (Instituto de Aposentadoria e Pensões dos Bancários – IAPB), and recognizing the employees of the Audit Committee of the Institute of Retirement and Pensions of Industry Employees (Conselho Fiscal do Instituto de Aposentadoria e Pensões dos Industriários).

In January 1954, Jango began studies for review of the minimum wage, facing two types of pressure: the mobilization of workers in larger cities to claim a readjustment of 100% that would increase the minimum wage from Cr$ 1,200.00 to Cr$2,400.00, and entrepreneurs' refusal to review the policy since the Eurico Gaspar Dutra administration, which allegedly contributed to the impoverishment of several segments of the Brazilian society. The business community said that it would agree to a 42% raise in the minimum wage to match the cost of living in 1951. On May Day, Vargas signed the new minimum wage into law, which was a 100% increase as demanded by the working class.

Jango resigned as labor minister in February 1954, passing the job to his legal substitute Hugo de Faria, and resumed his term as a deputy, as a result of the strong reaction of the media and military against the new minimum wage.

The political crisis of the Vargas administration deepened after one of his bodyguards was involved in an assassination attempt against UDN leader Carlos Lacerda on 5 August 1954. Vargas was put under pressure by the media, which demanded his resignation. On 24 August 1954 at 1 a.m., Vargas called Jango to Catete Palace and handed him a document to be read only after he arrived back in Rio Grande do Sul. It was his suicide letter.

Vice President

Vice President Goulart (right) at the inauguration of Juscelino Kubitschek on 31 January 1956.

After Vargas' suicide, Jango thought about leaving politics forever. However, at the president's burial on 26 August 1954, he seemed to have given up the idea, declaring that "we, within the law and order, we'll know how to fight with patriotism and dignity, inspired by the example that you [Vargas] left us."

In October 1954, elections were held for the Federal Senate, the Chamber of Deputies, state governments, and state assemblies. The second half of the year started off with uncertainties for the PTB and its allies. Emotionally and politically shaken by attacks made by Vargas' rivals, Jango departed from political activities for a few weeks. He only returned after a series of meetings with PTB leaders in Rio Grande do Sul. By the end of these meetings, it was decided that Jango would run for the Senate. However, both Jango and fellow PTB leader Ruy Ramos (two seats were being contested) were defeated. The PTB also lost the gubernatorial election in Rio Grande do Sul, although it was able to elect a large number of deputies in both the State Assembly and Chamber of Deputies.

In November 1954, the PTB and PSD began to discuss an electoral coalition for the 1955 elections. Minas Gerais governor Juscelino Kubitschek was PSD's choice for the Presidency. On 7 November, Kubitschek gave an interview suggesting a coalition between the two parties. His candidacy was approved by the Minas Gerais branch of the party at the end of November. After this, discussions took place regarding the selection of his vice-presidential candidate. After troubled negotiations, João Goulart, whom he had initially proposed, was chosen. The PSD National Convention was held on 10 February 1955, with the confirmation of Kubitschek as the party's presidential candidate.

Meanwhile, Vargas' vice president Café Filho formed a government with several UDN ministers, which impeded governance, and proved himself uncommitted with the latter President's government plans. In December 1954, Juarez Távora, his chief of military staff, threatened to veto Jango as a vice-presidential candidate. In April 1955, the National Directory of PSD accepted the nomination of Jango, and in the same month, the alliance was approved by the PTB National Convention. The candidacy was ready but vulnerable to new vetoes of Jango in the military and among dissident leaders of PSD.

After the PTB National Convention, a letter from Brazilian Communist Party (Partido Comunista Brasileiro – PCB) leader Luiz Carlos Prestes to Jango was published in the press. In the letter, Prestes suggested that PTB and PCB could work together for the benefit of the Brazilian population. That was enough to intensify the actions of those plotting a coup. In addition to the smear campaign run by Carlos Lacerda in his newspaper *Tribuna da Imprensa* and the usual plotting inside the military, April ended with a statement by former president Dutra in *O Globo* opposing Jango's candidacy. From the institutional point of view, the crisis did not have major repercussions, and the PSD ratified its support for Goulart as Kubitschek's running mate at a convention in June, even with the dissent of the party in Rio Grande do Sul, Santa Catarina, and Pernambuco.

In 1956, Goulart was elected vice president, as the running mate of president Kubitschek. Goulart was re-elected vice president in 1960. As vice president, he also served as president of the Senate.[7] However, the 1960 election gave the presidency to Jânio Quadros, a member of a different party. At the time, Brazilians could vote for different tickets for president and vice president. Quadros resigned in 1961 because he no longer had a majority in the National Congress of Brazil.

The Goulart administration

Goulart with U.S. President John F. Kennedy during a visit to the United States in April 1962.

Goulart was out of the country on a state visit to China when Quadros resigned. Several political and military elements thought Goulart was too radical for the presidency. They objected to his left-wing tendencies, his nationalist policies, and his willingness to seek closer relations with Communist countries. These elements called for the vice presidency to be declared vacant so new elections could be held.

Congress was initially reluctant to recognize Goulart as president. He returned to Brazil a few days after Quadros' resignation, insisting he was already president. A compromise was agreed upon, thanks to Leonel Brizola and the "cadeia de legalidade" (chain of legality), and Goulart was able to take the presidency, but with his powers constrained by a parliamentary system of government.

A constitutional amendment was accordingly passed which transferred most of the president's powers to the newly created post of prime minister. Only after this amendment was Goulart allowed to take the oath of office as president, to serve as head of state only. Goulart nominated Tancredo Neves as prime minister.

During this period, Goulart and his prime minister chose the three-year plan as the economic plan of his government under the advisement of Celso Furtado, his minister of planning. In order to strengthen the energy sector and to foster Brazilian development, Eletrobrás, Latin America's largest power utility company, was created in 1962.

As part of the compromise that installed a parliamentary system of government in 1961, a plebiscite was set for 1963 to confirm or reverse the changes made to the constitution. The parliamentary system of government was overwhelmingly rejected in the referendum, and Goulart assumed full presidential powers.

The presidential government of Goulart initiated in 1963 was marked politically by the administration's closer ties to center-left political groups, and conflict with more conservative sectors of the society, specifically the National Democratic Union.

Goulart also led Brazil in the drive for a nuclear-free Latin America, providing the impetus for the Five

Presidents' Declaration and the Treaty of Tlatelolco. Brazil's leadership on nuclear disarmament was a casualty of the military coup, and Mexico eventually stepped in to continue to drive for a nuclear-free region.[8]

Goulart during a ticker tape parade in New York City, 1962.

Basic reforms

Goulart's Basic Reforms plan (*Reformas de Base*) was a group of social and economic measures of nationalist character that ushered in a greater state intervention in the economy. Among the reforms were:

- Education reform to combat adult illiteracy, with the widespread use of the pioneering teachings and method of Paulo Freire. The government also proposed to hold a university reform and prohibited the operation of private schools. Fifteen percent of Brazil's income would be directed to education.

- Tax reform to control the transfer of profits by multinational companies with headquarters abroad, instead reinvesting profits in Brazil. The income tax would be proportional to personal profit.

- Electoral reform to extend voting rights to illiterate people and low-ranking military officers.

- Land reform to expropriate and redistribute non-productive properties larger than 600 hectares to the population. At that time, the agricultural population was larger than the urban population.

The military coup

Main article: 1964 Brazilian coup d'état

Goulart and his wife Maria Teresa during the March 13, 1964 speech

In the early hours of 31 March 1964, General Olímpio Mourão Filho, in charge of the 4th Military Region, headquartered in Juiz de Fora, Minas Gerais, ordered his troops to start moving toward Rio de Janeiro to depose Goulart.[9]

On 1 April, at 12:45 p.m., João Goulart left Rio for the capital, Brasília, in an attempt to stop the coup politically. [10] When he reached Brasília, Goulart realized that he lacked any political support. The Senate president, Auro Moura Andrade, was already calling for congressional support of the coup. Goulart stayed for a short time in

Brasília, gathering his wife and two children, and flying to Porto Alegre in an Air Force Avro 748 aircraft. Soon after Goulart's plane took off, Auro Moura Andrade declared the position of President of Brazil "vacant".[11]

In the first hours of 2 April, Auro Moura de Andrade, along with the president of the Supreme Federal Court, swore in Pascoal Ranieri Mazzilli, the speaker of the house, as president. This move was arguably unconstitutional at the time, as João Goulart was still in the country.[12]

At the same time, Goulart, now in the headquarters of the 3rd Army in Porto Alegre, still loyal to him at the time, contemplated resistance and counter-moves with Leonel Brizola, who argued for armed resistance. In the morning, General Floriano Machado informed the president that troops loyal to the coup were moving from Curitiba to Porto Alegre and that he had to leave the country, otherwise risking arrest. At 11:45 am, Goulart boarded a Douglas C-47 transport for his farm bordering Uruguay. Goulart would stay on his farmland until 4 April, when he finally boarded the plane for the last time, heading for Montevideo.[13]

The coup installed successive right-wing hardliners as heads of state who suspended civil rights and liberties of the Brazilian people.[14] They abolished all political parties and replaced them with only two, the military government's party called the National Renewal Alliance Party (Aliança Renovadora Nacional – ARENA) and the consented opposition Brazilian Democratic Movement

(Movimento Democrático Brasileiro – MDB). The MDB, however, had no real power, and the military rule was marked by widespread disappearance, torture, and exile of many politicians, university students, writers, singers, painters, filmmakers, and other artists.

President João Goulart was not favorably viewed in Washington. He took an independent stance in foreign policy, resuming relations with socialist countries and opposing sanctions against Cuba; his administration passed a law limiting the amount of profits multinationals could transmit outside the country; a subsidiary of ITT was nationalized; he promoted economic and social reforms.

Lincoln Gordon served as U.S. Ambassador to Brazil (1961–66), where he played a major role for the support of the opposition against the government of President João Goulart and during the 1964 Brazilian *coup d'état*. On 27 March 1964, he wrote a top secret cable to the US government, urging it to support the coup of Humberto de Alencar Castello Branco with a "clandestine delivery of arms" and shipments of gas and oil, to possibly be supplemented by CIA covert operations. Gordon believed that Goulart, wanting to "seize dictatorial power," was working with the Brazilian Communist Party. Gordon wrote: "If our influence is to be brought to bear to help avert a major disaster here--which might make Brazil the China of the 1960s--this is where both I and all my senior advisors believe our support should be placed." In the years after the coup, Gordon, Gordon's staff, and the CIA repeatedly denied that they had been involved, and President Lyndon B. Johnson praised Gordon's service in Brazil as "a rare combination of experience and scholarship, idealism and practical judgment." In 1976, Gordon stated that the Johnson Administration "had been prepared to intervene militarily to prevent a leftist takeover of the government," but did not directly state that it had or had not intervened.

Circa 2004 many documents were declassified and placed online at the GWU National Security Archive, indicating the involvement of Johnson, McNamara, Gordon, and others. In 2005, Stansfield Turner's book described the involvement of ITT Corporation president Harold Geneen and CIA Director John McCone. Attorney General Robert F. Kennedy was uneasy about Goulart allowing "communists" to hold positions in government agencies. US President Lyndon Johnson and his Defense Secretary Robert S. McNamara were also worried.[15] Kennedy, who had made plans for the coup when his brother John was President, characterized Goulart as a "wily" politician in a White House tape.[16]

The president of ITT, Harold Geneen, was a friend of the Director of Central Intelligence, John McCone. Between 1961 and 1964,[16] the CIA performed psyops against Goulart, performed character assassination, pumped money into opposition groups, and enlisted the help of the Agency for International Development and the AFL-CIO.[15] It has also been acknowledged that the Kennedy Administration was the architect of the coup and that President Johnson inherited plans for it.[16] US President John F. Kennedy had discussed options on how to deal with Goulart with Gordon and his chief Latin America advisor Richard N. Goodwin in July 1962 and determined in December 1962 that the coup was necessary in order to advance US interests.[16]

Life in exile

João Goulart in 1964

On 4 April 1964, Jango and his family landed in Uruguay seeking political asylum. After his first years in Montevideo, he bought a farm on the Uruguay-Brazil border, where he devoted himself to farming cattle. In 1966 he took part in the Frente Ampla (*Broad Front*) political movement, which aimed to fully restore democratic rule in Brazil through peaceful means. The end of Frente Ampla also resulted in the end of Jango's political activity. He decided to focus on managing his farms located in Uruguay, Paraguay, Argentina, and Brazil.

In late 1973, Argentine president Juan Domingo Perón invited Jango to live in Buenos Aires and asked him to collaborate on a plan to expand Argentine meat exports to Europe and other markets that would not traditionally buy the Argentine commodity. However, Perón's minister of social welfare and private secretary José López Rega opposed the designation. Nevertheless, Jango decided to stay in Buenos Aires.

In March 1976 in the town of La Plata, the Argentine Army dismantled a group of right-wing terrorists planning to kidnap Jango's son and demand a high ransom in cash. With his personal security compromised, the former president distanced himself from Buenos Aires. This experience led Jango to arrange new steps for his safe return to Brazil. However, this was delayed because of upcoming elections.

Death

On 6 December 1976, Goulart died in his apartment La Villa, in the Argentine municipality of Mercedes, province of Corrientes, supposedly of a heart attack. Since Goulart's body was not submitted to an autopsy, the cause of his death is unconfirmed. Around 30,000 people attended his funeral service, which was censored from press coverage by the military dictatorship.

On 26 April 2000, the former governor of Rio Grande do

Sul and Rio de Janeiro, Leonel Brizola, said that former presidents Goulart and Kubitschek were assassinated as part of Operation Condor and requested investigations into their deaths.[17][18]

Goulart's remains arrive in Brasília for exhumation, almost 40 years after his death, 14 November 2013.

On 27 January 2008, the newspaper *Folha de S. Paulo* printed a story with a statement from Mario Neira Barreiro, a former intelligence service member under Uruguay's dictatorship. Barreiro said that Goulart was poisoned, confirming Brizola's allegations. Barreiro also said that the order to assassinate Goulart came from Sérgio Paranhos Fleury, head of the Departamento de Ordem Política e Social (Department of Political and Social Order), and the license to kill came from president Ernesto Geisel.[19][20] In July 2008, a special commission of the legislative assembly of Rio Grande do Sul, Goulart's home state, concluded that "the evidence that Jango was willfully assassinated, with knowledge of the Geisel government, is strong."[21]

In March 2009, the magazine *CartaCapital* published previously unreleased documents of the National

Intelligence Service, created by an undercover agent who was present at Jango's properties in Uruguay. This revelation reinforces the theory that the former president was poisoned. The Goulart family has not yet identified who could be the "B Agent" that is mentioned in the documents. The agent acted as a close friend to Jango and described in detail an argument during the former president's 56th birthday party with his son stemming from a fight between two employees.[22] As a result of the story, the Human Rights Commission of the Chamber of Deputies decided to investigate Jango's death.[23]

Later, *CartaCapital* published an interview with Jango's widow, Maria Teresa Fontela Goulart, who revealed documents from the Uruguayan government that documented her complaints that her family was being monitored. The Uruguayan government was monitoring Jango's travel and his business and political activities. These files were from 1965, a year after the coup in Brazil, and suggest that he could have been deliberately attacked. The Movement for Justice and Human Rights and the President João Goulart Institute have requested a document in which the Uruguayan interior ministry said that "serious and responsible Brazilian sources" talked about an "alleged plot against the former Brazilian president."[24]

Political views

Afro-Brazilians

Closeness to poor people, especially poor Afro-Brazilians, was a normal behavior for the young Jango. The main leader of his Carnival block *Comigo Ninguém Pode*, mãe-de-santo Jorgina Vieira, declared in an interview with the newspaper *Zero Hora* that Jango was one of the only white boys of São Borja to be a member of the block. In a particular Carnival celebration in the 1940s, he broke the high society rules and led the block inside the aristocratic Clube Comercial, which would not allow blacks in their halls until the late 1960s.

Communism

Like many other leftist politicians of the Cold War era, Jango was accused of being a communist at various times. As a response to Carlos Lacerda, his most frequent accuser, he cited right-wing politicians also supported by the Brazilian Communist Party whom the latter would not criticize. In an interview with the newspaper *O Jornal*, Jango declared: "regarding the communists, they have supported indistinctly candidates of several political affiliations, conservatives or populists. I do not wish to distinguish such support, but I will only allow myself this question: is perhaps Colonel Virgílio Távora a communist, just because, ostensibly, he accepts the support of communists in Ceará? How to say that the illustrious patriot of UDN Milton Campos is communist, for accepting, as he did in Minas, the same votes requested by Mr. Afonso Arinos here in Rio?"

Tributes and amnesty

In 1984, exactly twenty years after the coup, filmmaker Sílvio Tendler directed a documentary chronicling Jango's political career through archive footage and interviews with influential politicians. *Jango* was viewed in theaters by over half a million people, becoming the sixth-largest grossing Brazilian documentary. It was critically acclaimed, receiving three awards at the Gramado Film Festival and one at the Havana Film Festival, as well as the Silver Daisy, given by the National Conference of Brazilian Bishops (Conferência Nacional dos Bispos do Brasil).

There are at least ten schools throughout Brazil named after Goulart. Most are located on Rio Grande do Sul, in the municipalities of Alvorada, Ijuí, Novo Hamburgo, Porto Alegre, Viamão, and in Jango's native São Borja. There are three schools named after Jango in Rio de Janeiro, Balneário Camboriú and Santa Catarina, and another in São João de Meriti in Rio de Janeiro. On 6 December 2007, exactly 31 years after Goulart's death, a monument was erected in Balneário Camboriú depicting Jango sitting on a bench on the Avenida Atlântica (in front of the Atlantic Ocean) with his two children. It was designed by artist Jorge Schroder upon the request of mayor Rubens Spernau.

On 28 June 2008, the Avenida Presidente João Goulart

(President João Goulart Avenue) in Osasco was inaugurated in São Paulo.[25] The boulevard is about 760 meters long and is the first of the city with a bicycle path. Other cities, such as Canoas, Caxias do Sul, Cuiabá, Lages, Pelotas, Porto Alegre, Porto Velho, Ribeirão Preto, Rio de Janeiro, Rondonópolis, São Borja, São Leopoldo, São Paulo, and Sobral already have roads honoring Jango.

On 15 November 2008, Jango and his widow Maria Teresa received political amnesty from the federal government at the 20th National Congress of Lawyers in Natal, Rio Grande do Norte. The former First Lady received a restitution of R$ 644,000 (around US$322,000) to be paid in pensions of R$5,425 (around US$2,712) per month for Jango having been restrained from practicing as a lawyer. She also received a restitution of R$100,000 (around US$50,000) for the 15 years in which her family was forbidden to return to Brazil.[26]

> It will never be enough emphasize the heroic role of Jango to the Brazilian people, given that he represents as few do the ideal of a fairer, more egalitarian, and more democratic Brazil. (…) The government recognizes its mistakes of the past and apologizes to a man who defended the nation and its people; a man whom we could not have done without.
>
> — Letter by Lula da Silva to the Amnesty Commission.[27]

Boy at Ipanema

"We are going to borrow someone else's kid when we have dinner with the president of Brazil, and we will leave you on the beach in your own room to do whatever you please," said my father.

My father had brought me with him to Cuzco, Peru where we walked up a long hot dry hill almost breathless to a Cathedral where he knocked on the door and inquired about the presence of a certain monk.

"Oh no, he's no longer here!" insisted the priest angrily while trying to close the door on my father's invading shoe polished very well like they do that in the Navy.

Evidently we were inquiring about a monk rumored to be Martin Borman, Hitler's adjutant general. He had fled that monastery at the request of the U.S. State Department for more fatchist friendly Asuncion, Paraguay only to catch Yellow Fever and die there. Another rumor perhaps that one is.

Yet now on Ipanema where I had a very cheap motel room that was the best one offered, I waved goodbye not terribly affectionately as I had been ditched for the presidential dinner where I might spill the beans about my father's being a U.S. Agent not a tobacco tsar like his brothers in Connecticut.

The Brazilian girls on the beach informed me that their boyfriends were coming after dark to kill me if they would find me with them. So I took their advice and wandered into the suburbs to attend all night drinking parties at several big rich mansions as it goes on like that in Rio De Janeiro nightly.

Meanwhile my father and stepmother, Dorothy, attended an extravagant state sponsored dinner with the newly elected leftist Brazilian president whose child entertained my father's replacement child with my name surely. They wandered freely in the compound those children playing games etcetera. From my impostor replacement and his memory of that evening were drawn detailed maps of the entire compound for the right wing junta that toppled the government one year later.

The Accident

Okay you must realize our government has covert operations' Our government has covert funds that go to undisclosed top secret operatives to fund assassins overseas or in some cases domestic threats. Bang bang bang. Your taxes at wok. Bang bang bang. There are corrupt cops with too much power who get freedy like J. Edgar Hoover. Maybe Jimmy Hoffa the teamsters got too powerful. Bang bang bang. It doesn't pay to be greedy. Bang bang bang.

Upon occasion then there might arise a politician who has had some experience with this element of government. He thinks he can walk down Madison Avenue and bang bang bang. No one's gonna prosecute him cause he'sd a rich son-of-a -bitch.

There are the Democrats all goody little two shoes straight as arrows. I doubt it. Maybe without so much money they are not in position to sponsor the hit. Why should we trust them? Every newer day they are moving a step closer to Communism.

Okay now you got Trump losing the election and losing power but what did the Republicans do to Ed Muskie? They mickeyed his drink and he went to give a big speech and wept like a baby. End of him.

So there I was in North Conway where I learned

too much too fast and there was Tyler Palmer's neighbor Rick Jordan, son of a chemist from St. Louis who was aspiring to be a chemist himself.

There is some local young lady with really big teats. She dyes her hair blond because she is an Arab but good looking. She goes to Washington, D.C. and sleeps with some Senators as a "Call Girl" makes those naughty films to sell for a profit. She is in the fast lane so she joins Al Qaeda too as they promise her money and a chance to visit the homeland and see the world.

She flies home to North Conway. She wants to be like Belle Star in the movie" How the West was won. Bang bang bang. She wants to shoot some guy snoring too loud through the wall. Sleep forever! Bang bang bang.

She offers me some cookies she baked. But I already ate the one with ten hits of LSD maybe by mistake, who knows?

Elsie Limmer and Stephanie and this Atab girl all work for this guy Tick Jordan making all these little pills at the (covert) factory on Conway Lake.

So which worthless dissident hippie they gonna kill for Nixon tonight or tomorrow?

The Arab girl has a gun in her purse in case something goes wrong. She's gonna fix it like Belle Star. poor naive baby. Everybody has been to this movie before. They all have experience at least as much or more than she.

Rick Jordan waits there on the side of that mountain. Somebody's gonna die. Your taxes at work! She pulls out her gun and points it at his head,

"Eat my pussy!" she screams, "Then I'm gonna blow your brains out!"

They tumble down the mountain wrestling over the gun but she is a woman and more frail. She breaks her neck.

Shit happens in this rotten world where gravity sucks. Everybody gonna see his/her Maker on the Judgement Day. You too gonna stand in front of the Judge.

"Son, are you trying to tell me that you conspired to kill your own father and that therefore he retaliated and tried to kill you?"

"I was drunk, your Honour."

That will never hold up in Court. Better it would be if you would have remained sober and never have been a hippy in the first place, son!"

"Yes, Father.

Grateful

Dear Francis Tansey and all the Mountain Dew and Vertical Crew over the thirty seasons,

I sincerely thank each and all of you for my excellent and wonderful adventure at your events for thirty years. This year I will hopefully reach my goal of three hundred medals (236 alpine and 64 snowboard). It was great fun for a great cause "Make-a-wish" which has raised so much money to help the handicapped and disabled children fight their battles against debilitating diseases and handicaps.

Here is my list of the ski areas attended: Monarch, Powderhorn, Breckenridge, Camelback, Jack Frost, Big Boulder, Catamount, Whiteface(I missed both as my furnace quit), Jiminy Peak, Nashoba, Bradford, Ski Ward, Butternut, Mt Snow, Bromley, Stratton, Okemo, Killington, Sugarbush, Suicide Six, Pico, Sugarbush North(Glen Ellen), Smuggler's Notch, Bolton Valley, Stowe(I missed that one, my car broke down and with my dog I was stranded in ten degree temperatures until five o'clock when the sun had set in Montpelier). Jay Peak, Saddleback, Black Mt(ME), Sunday River, Shawnee Peak (Mt Pleasant). Mt Abrams, Sugarloaf(I missed), Lost Valley, Cranmore, Wildcat, Mt Attitash, Tenney Mountain, Ragged Mountain, Waterville Valley,

Cannon Mt, Dartmouth Skiway, Mount Sunapee, Crotched Mountain, Gunstock, Black Mt(NH), Pats Peak, Mount Southington(CT), Berkshire East(MA), what was that called The Irish Alps MA, I think if there is still time left let's have one at Yawgoo, RI?

I competed in 44 out of 47 mentioned but missed four more in Pennsylvania. I must have won an average of seven podiums at each resort including fifteen times at a few. I did this mostly with my compatriot Brian "Hans" Pendleton, the ex Burke Mountain Ski Patroller while I was also an ex ski instructor at several resorts. Is there any way to describe this joy of a day at the ski races where one finds oneself a totally thoroughbred race horse charging out of the gate onto the race track at a full gallop!!?!!

I didn't always podium and neither did Pendleton. So actually we race 700 times at least.

I know you raced the NCAA's and the Olympics too but you probably didn't race almost four hundred starts plus of course I raced the beer leagues with greats like GP Houston and David Blampied and Tyler Palmer, Okay that;s another 700 starts. This was all after I was on the US SKi Team for one minute and a day. I didn't last there very long only as long as the joy held out. I think the US Ski Team had financial problems and needed willing parents to support it lavishly.

Dear Dad, Thank you, your less than fully obedient son, Duncan. PS Yes, I will think about growing up some day but I am in no hurry as I am having too much fun in mostly New England and neighboring states with Frank Tansey and the gang (his crew).

So I am truly grateful even though I never served and was 4A exempt from the draft as my father was a CIA and I was kidnapped by Argentine Special Forces(Otto S.). More about that later. No, that was not so much fun but I did get to ski race in the Andes,

Yes this has been a whole lifetime of high adventure and thrills even though I passed up on the all night downhill event at King Pine to raise more money for charity. Maybe I had gotten too old for that sort of overnight camping on a chairlift. Lol.

If you work at a desk, forgive me, I never graduated from college, pushed a mop in high school and also worked at a factory at night still in high school plus a farm still in high school.

So I really thought about it, especially about what Emerson and Thoreau said about the Child being father of the Man. It made sense to me to just keep being a Child of God and the ski lift or just walk up through the woods if you can't buy a lift ticket. That's why I am still grateful, all those hikes up through the woods at Mountain Dew Vertical Challenge now also Pepsi or Coca Cola Challenge plus Chevy, Ocean Spray, Fischer Skis, Muscle Milk, Granola, Dannon, I'm sorry I can't remember all the sponsors but joyfully buy all their products willingly and I'm so happy I wasn't born in the USSR, Amen

America and Vertical Challenge are both still great and complement one another. God bless America and please if you can make it come and participate or just to watch Vertical Challenge, Francis Tansey and his marvelous Crew. We are all in this together and God willing we will win! That is today's great lesson brought to you by all our great sponsors of family skiing.

Be safe. Be well, and see you on the slopes of the USA!

Gerry Knapp aka "The Knapper"

I was still a child at Bromley Mountain in Vermont when my father, struggling with his Stem Christies and I in my Snowplow Schuss going straight down encountered a bamboo slalom course set for the Rice family, father and two sons. They all wore those old slalom hats with ear flaps and visors like baseball hats but made of leather not cotton. The slalom poles had little flags attached of three colors, blue, red and yellow. It looked like fun so I skied by a few of those flags in imitation but was soon yelled at to stay off their course. It was a wake up call that skiing was for the rich and Anglo-Saxon my father told me but added that Austrians were by far the very best skiers on this planet.

At Prep school I felt some of the same prejudice when issued my first jumping skis, the bear trap bindings of which were mounted two inches behind center of my pair which no one took notice of three dismal weeks during which my ski tips dropped upon takeoff and I landed and cartwheeled on the knoll. my ski jumping career was not looking very promising as I was immensely discouraged and soaking wet with my clothes full of snow from back to back crashes.

My roommate that first year at Holderness was a Pakistani who prayed every early morning to Mecca, a faraway place where Allah was God. Eventually I would teach him to fight our English teacher, Fleck from Bowdoin College in Maine where just white people went to school.

The winners of the Eastern Junior Championships were all Anglo-Saxon, Irish or French Canadian American. It, skiing, was the last great white hope with blond Penny Pitou from Gunstock, NH winning silver medals in the Squaw Valley Olympics. White people everywhere had money and sportscars and went skiing on weekends. Nonwhite people lived in Ghettos and their children played basketball, track and just a few were inducted into baseball where Mickey Mantle was my favorite until Hank Aaron hit that ninth inning home run to beat the New York Yankees. Hank Aaron was dark as night itself. Then the So-Jo kid Willie Mays ran deep into the box in center field and caught a deep fly ball hit over his head that no white person had ever attempted to catch in that fashion and the Giants won the World Series.

There were some tough and mean boxers who were also African American but nobody dared say anything about racism in sports until Cassius Clay changed his name to Mohammed Ali. I never should have listened to him as identifying with those poor underdogs gave me some strength but led me into an identity crisis with my Anglo-Saxon teammates on the US Ski Team who presumed I was not Catholic nor pure white. It was my young undeveloped immature brain which detested them like the Rice Brothers who had yelled at me to stay off their Anglo-Saxon slalom course.

I wanted to ski and I wanted to win slalom races because deep down inside me there was a fighter and losing was not in my nature.

"Hi, I'm Gerry, get in the car!" said Gerry Knapp who was also a ski racer. He was from Stowe at least temporarily as his sister had moved there and married a mob boss he said.

"Really?" I was naive. Why would a mob boss live in Stowe I wondered, having seen them mostly on television or on newsreals at the theater.

Gerry Knapp was older than me by four years chronologically but from a very wise races, Jewish Yugoslav and some Saxon back there somewhere, the Knapps were Austrian. So we had a lot in common racing against the Anglo-0Saxon rich kids many of whom were raised work ethic Saxon and soon dropped out of the sport to take jobs, marry and raise children. Not us ski bums, we were enjoying the sport too much and Gerry said,

"Take a hit of this reefer" and I did but it wasn't my first. Rebel Ryan passed me my first joint in Boulder, Colorado two years before then we dragged a thirty foot horizontal Christmas Tree into the house through several doorways until it became stuck and the doors wouldn't close.

"How much money did you bring with you?" Gerry asked me somewhere near Indiana on our drive out west to go race Aspen and Steamboat in the national races called the Wild West Classic, Bear Valley CA, Jackson Hole WY Steamboat CO etc.

Well I have twenty two cans of Kippered snacks

*in tin cans) and whoops only seven dollars. We were indeed the poor kids en route to race the rich white kids.

"O my God'said Gerry and mused a while then stopped for gas and coffee.

"I'm not going to kick you out of my car here in the middle of nowhere," he finally replied adding,

"Do you have some friends out west where we can stay when we get there in Aspen?"

"Well, my friend John Stirling has a place near Carbondale on Missouri Heights... and I have a girlfriend who is going to school in Steamboat if we get there named Wendy Coughlin."

We arrived in Steamboat where Wendy said on the phone to wait till after dark and use the hidden ladder to climb into her second floor dorm window. She got expelled for that eventually but said college didn't agree with her life style anyway.

At the end of that long ski racing season the Knapper showed up in North Conway and said,

"Get in my car" I did.

He then added that I owed him and he was instructed by his bosses to drive me to Stowe non stop because "They" wanted me not to race in the final race of the year, the Mount Washington American Inferno. I didn't try and jump out because I knew I had to go retrieve a Peugeot racing bicycle in Stowe that had been delivered to my client but not paid for.

"Well if you are down and out with no money and no career and no future you can always join the family" said the man in Stowe from behind his thick glasses at the kitchen table.

The next morning at five o'clock I found my way out of the house and had that bicycle somehow maybe someone dropped it off for me. It was April 23,1969 and twenty six degrees with a dusting of snow on the road and I escaped en route to plymouth, NH 110 miles away and got within 25 miles my hands all frozen and somebody made a telephone call and John French came and picked me up wondering just what in hell I was up to.

The next morning after a six thirty breakfast I began pedaling toward Meredith, NH where frozen again I called Wendy Bryant in North Conway my landlord who sent Danny Del Rossi to pick me up on the highway in Chocorua, NH on my bicycle. It was two days before the Inferno Ski race. My frozen hands would possibly have time to heal.

The Very Last Amateurs

I would like to describe us as the very last of the amateurs. We were encamped on the side of Mount Washington just below lower "Lower Snowfields' ‹ on the flats there were sometimes the river backs up and floods if it rains for over a day. Skippy, my companion and friend, had found the army tent somewhere or borrowed it. It had no floor but there were spruce bows for that. Most of that very well tented area had been denuded of the lower branches of all Spruce trees. Nowadays that's not the case as the U.S. Forest Service has banned camping up there since 1969 but it was 1968 when I had made my triumphal return to that Mount Washington which taught me how to ski modern.

Due to the grace and benevolence of my father (who had adopted me) I had received ski lessons and ski coaching from "Miki" Clemens Hutter from Salzburg, Austria. He taught me to Ski The Austrian Way "Wedeln" as it was written by Kruckenhauser" who preached skis in parallel as the only correct technique. Mount Washington albeit Tuckerman's Ravine and Hillman's Highway were teaching me differently.

From our tent location below Dodge's Drop we could see ski tracks up there carved by Brooks Dodge who had finished fourth place in the 1956 Olympic Slalom.

If I would have known that at the time I would have followed him everywhere even though our introduction to one another one time had not gone well.

Nobody paid Brooks Dodge to ski those death defying chutes, and nobody was paying me either. I was not yet twenty one and not of legal age at twenty to inherit anything. Skipper spent most of each day listening to various skier's big adventure stories and smiling enthusiastically but adding his last line as they packed their belongings to head down the mountainside for home,

"You don't have to carry all that heavy food home with you unless of course you must!"

Very well spoken by Skipper (Franklin Corning Stevens, Jr) at least five times daily. Albeit four out of five departing mountaineers would leave us their food but not their beer very often. So for beer which was one commodity necessary for Skipper we went to town once a week or whenever it ran out. There was also an Arab down there in North Conway named "Woody" who it was rumored worked for "The Man". We did odd jobs upon occasion for Woody to earn beer money such as clearing building lots and burning brush but it was usually a Korean War Vet named Chet that ran the chain saw. Chet thought I looked like a gook as I had the high set eyebrows and or high cheekbones like an American Indian or something. I stayed away from Chet as the war had made him nuts.

"That wasn't a war, Chet! That was the Korean "Conflict". You wouldn't want to say that too loudly to Chet's face.

So then me and Skipper Skippy Stevens took turns lugging the two cases of beer back up the mountainside. Sometimes Skippy sold a single can for $5 which was the going price at 5000 ft elevation. We only once climbed to the 6,288 ft summit as the weather up there turned deadly with high wind and below freezing temperatures even in late May. Of course the snow mostly melted by June and so we left for the lowlands of the Conways wear the girls our age were putting on tennis snorts and bathing suits to dip in Lake Conway.

Thus in the spring of 1968 I only lived at Tuckerman Ravine ten weeks and skied on average 2-4 runs per day about five days per week. We sat a lot in the lunch rocks and drank beer, Skippy five to my one probably. I made over eighty or ninety ski runs on Mount Washington that one spring the year before the 1969 Mount Washington Inferno Ski Race held for the first time since 1939 as the weather on the summit of that mountain was never very cooperative.

There were some young girls who would spend the night with me there in my sleeping bag though the very next morning they usually departed without skiing to find a hot bath at home in the valley below. Our accommodations were primitive at best and because people urinated in the dark of night without venturing very far into the woods we often had to move the tent to a fresher smelling location. Of course the U.S. Forest Service put an end to us mountainside residents as the environment was being ecologically upset albeit the Hell's Angel Motorcycle Club some chapter of it began camping out up there maybe dirty yards away through the woods dropping LSD and other drugs as well. We knew Richard Nixon and the various powers like Harvard University and Ski Club had a dismal view of most most motorcycle affectionados without college degrees

James and John

They were Jamie Arnold and John Stirling. They both were ski racers like me, they both loved their dogs as much as their women; I went with them to the Colorado Cup at Winter Park in February. They both enjoyed reefers, long cigarettes of marijuana that everyone in Aspen rolled into "Joints" as that was the new trend in those days to be like "The Beatl;es" in England, long haired rock stars on the world's fresh stage.

Certainly we all were ourselves on that glorious day. I had already won the Steamboat classic slalom while being threatened with disqualification if I would wear my dirty blue jeans in the second run by the chief of course, U.S. Men's National Ski coach, a cowboy named Bill Marolt. His uncle was Max Marolt of Aspen who would one day die of a heart attack in Las Lenas, Argentina taking too many non-stop runs in a row without resting and drinking enough water. So I promptly put on my ski pants for the second run then to win that race.

Luckily here at Winter Park it was a different set of race officials as we were all stoned out of our minds from the pot which was much stronger than we had smoked in quite a while, maybe "Panama Red".

In any case I had narrowly won the first run after

John Stirling insisted I eat a huge pancake breakfast to satisfy my Id so it would not trick my Ego by rebellion, hooking a ski tip on a slalom gate or somesuch. John Stirling was reading back to back books by Gurdiyev and Ouspensky called, "The Third Way" and filling me in on every minutest detail while passing a joint in the car,

"Smoke some more of this before the second run, it will calm your nerves!" Ha.

I remember Jamie James Arnold had fallen the first run after hooking a tip. He was more of a downhiller and didn't enjoy slalom and John was in fourth place as he had skied the permanent course I had set in the glade high on Sunlight ski area in the woods where we thought no one else would ever ski hopefully as our treed slalom up there had seven foot high ruts from making turns in fresh powder after each snowstorm. i think we only sideslipped it once the entire winter. some poor soul, a middle aged powder hound and probably a desk jockey skied upon it later that winter and hit a wall of snow breaking his leg. the Ski Patrol then launched an investigation into who had designed this hidden bobsled run among so many trees and a few chairlift witnesses had remembered seeing me and John in the vicinity. James knew better than to ski my suicide course, oh well.

So the second run me and John arrived at the start very relaxed almost to the point of falling over in the snowdrift and taking a short nap. I remember not pushing hard enough out of the starting gate but a very smooth run in all that freshly fallen snow I did have and managed to hang onto the lead by a tenth of a second ahead of Eric Poulsen and Dan

Mooney, both of California. My win propelled me into a tie for first place in the overall points for the High Country Trophy overall title for best skier in the Western USA. I am fairly sure that onlooking coaches from reputable colleges like Universities of Denver, Colorado and Wyoming knew exactly our exact game plan. We were the dirty hippies that their parents had been very afraid their own children might become and dropout of society altogether in a ski town like Aspen. John Stirling was anything but a dropout. He read Gurdiyev and Ouspensky on his every ride up every chair lift in existence plus an encyclopedia of every other book ever written. He was a subdivider of real estate and builder of fine homes on Missouri Heights that resembled Yankee Clippers that had grounded in Rocky Mountain foothills with copper roofs and marble sink tops. James Jamie Arnold was his first mate and top carpenter and I was their tag along laborer of sorts as I helped Joe Baldwin, their neighbor who pirated abandoned mines for every last thread of steel with his Burma jeep. Joe Baldwin was from Arkansas and was last seen a few years in a dead run for the summit of Mt Sopris, elevation 12,999 ft towering above 7000 ft Carbondale. Joe had taken a bit too much acid and kept running out of sight with everybody far behind. He was a follower of Ken Keasey, perhaps, and so died of a massive heart attack. John out of pity had sold him one of his cheapest least desirable building lots and Joe had built a gargantuan house that looked more like an erector set sprawled up a hillside in Clear Creek. His daughter lived there in the house with him after his wife had gone raving mad at him living there and runned off, maybe back to Arkansas. Colorado can be awfully cold in mid winter which lasts over seven months and a half. Summer is the 4rth of July until the 5th when it snows again in the high country.

John held onto fourth place narrowly missing a podium. He was a very strong fellow both a wrestler and boxer at University of Utah with his neighbor Carl Monahan whose daughter Kater made the U.S. Ski team a few years later being quite an attractive blond with good taste and a sharp dresser, very important with those fussy race officials.

Now I have told you some of the history of Missouri Heights in Carbondale which is rich and deep with John having three daughters by Ruthie, a Penn Dutch college grad from Philadelphia and a sharp dresser. James married and had a beautiful daughter by his second wife and worked himself to death as all carpenters do eventually. He is still driving his Mazda car with a Wankel jet engine spitting liquid gas out the tailpipe up in heaven. He finally sold that car as it lost power and with one good backfire might have self ignited and blown all its passengers out the front windows whichever. I sent a copy of my new book to James after he didn't reply to my phone call a year ago only to have his wife call me in the middle of the night to tell me he had passed away just last August. John too has left us prematurely in a car accident not his fault after he sailed around the world with Crazy Charlie and Olaf in the Sea of China where their ship was cut in half by a Soviet Destroyer in thick fog. They had all lived through that. We are not too long for this world. How sad but at least there is a rich folk history of all these very fine and dear people. I still and always will love them dearly and have so many fond memories of them. Rest in Peace my angels you were the saints…

Then we drove back to Aspen -Carbondale-Basalt stopping at a tavern which was the only business then where the giant keystone ski area and village now exists. John bought me a steak for his coaching me and my coaching him. I hadn't eaten in three weeks. Slalom skiers back then were very skinny starving beings like Larry Keenan, the Flash of Tabernash who had been winning the college ski Carnivals but quite often fell in the second run of any national slalom race. There were Gerry Shimer and Scott Pyles who would have won the overall as they not only won the giant slalom races but placed well in all the downhills. There were a lot of Californians like Craig "Doc" Halliday and "Bif" Gotchy, his sidekick. I will look up all their addresses but many have already passed to the angels as did Carl Monahan recently as well.

I had a mustache back then that I had cultivated to look like a Mexican just to psyche out the competition. The Denver Post, a right wing Republican newspaper quoted my former ski racing friend Roger Little of Montana as saying,

"Cullman is an Eastern flake, a good for nothing vagabond whose only knack is slalom because all the other racers fall in that event!" Thanks Roger for filling them all in with Western bias. We had been buddies once at the National Training Camp at Vail in

December. We often skied that course like a Chinese Downhill they call that when sometimes our skis even touched which made us laugh at sixty miles an hour as we were young and crazy back then…

Skiing in Peru part 2

The Nepalese high court finally decided that Mt Everest was created for man's enjoyment not vice versa.

Our newest sponsor is the manufacturer of these space suits, a private firm called BE THERE copyright Malcolm Lloyd MacBride2015. There have just been too many deaths on these high mountains and so much expense in retrieving bodies and these pressurized and atmosphere controlled suits will minimize the high risk. The suit however cannot save you if you fall skiing at 100 miles an hour and propel off a cliff. Finally my sleep is over, was I dreaming again? I better fetch my pen and write...

Skiing Without Skis

While snow-forecast on the internet predicts snow showers for Huascaran I will enjoy one day of downhill practice not on skis but at least with my ski poles running downhill from my neighborhood in the heights above Huaraz to the tourist agency downtown where the tour bus awaits its passengers and guide before the sun even rises over the massive Cordillera Blanca averaging 3.6 to 4.1 miles high

Ronaldhino

Ronaldinho was a dog.

His dog mother gave birth to him under a ski area cafeteria halfway up the ski slopes of Cerro Catedral, Alta Patagonia, Argentina.

When he was born he had no name at all other than puppy Cachetorrito.

"Arf, arf, arf," his mother called him with some barks.

Though for the simplicity of this story we will call him Ronaldinho because that is the name he received later in his life.

His mother dog was so hungry from pregnancy she had eaten some discarded chocolate bars left in the snow by very rich spoiled children from the capitol, Buenos Aires.

Later while nursing her puppies she ate another chocolate bar, not good for dogs because of the caffeine, not good for the puppies drinking her fresh milk with caffeine. The poor little puppies all became hyperactive and nervous to the extent that when the cook owner came to collect them and sell them at the market for a few Argentine pesos, Ronaldinho ran away into the mysterious beech forest on the high mountainside, El Bosque.

His mother dog came to nurse him once and tried to carry him back down the mountainside but he was already too heavy so she left him some discarded bones to chew. The young puppy was destined to be a wild dog.

Meanwhile a wolf mother lost one of her pups possibly to a condor, she was searching all night and day for it frantically when she discovered Ronaldinho whom she mistook for her own thinking he might have rolled in Guanaco turds as he now smelled different than her own pups but not much different.

But being a good wolf mother she brought the straggler puppy home to her wolf den where another of her puppies was now missing. At least she had Ronaldinho to nurse and mother.

So the young dog was very fortunate to have a mother at all since his own had gone with the cook to market in San Carlos de Bariloche, the nearest city. The cook became drunk on Chi Cha and lost all his money in a card game that lasted past midnight when supper was served.

The wolf mother brought all her cubs to a higher wolf den on Cerro Pillin on the other side of the mountain Catedral which is Vuriloche. The young Ronaldinho now became a tactical hunter in the footsteps of his mother. They ate shrews, moles, mice, marmots and sometimes dead things frozen in the snows of Pillin.

Once they even ate a dead skier who had skied a closed backcountry trail in the fog and had fallen off the backside of the mountain Catedral into Vuriloche. He was a big fat Porteno with a spare tire of lomo meat around his gargantuan belly. His family didn't even report him missing as he had spanked his wife and children continually so they did not miss him one iota.

Naughty big and naughty. The wolves and Ronaldinho now a wolf thought the fat porteno to be very delicious. Munch, munch, munch! There were many animals in the forest and fish Truchas in the ponds, lakes and rivers plus pumas (cougars) and condors and sea birds from the Pacific Ocean not to far away in Chile.

"What big eyes you have," said Ronaldinho to his wolf mother.

"All the better to see you with!" replied his wolf mother.

"What a big nose you have!" said Ronaldinho to his wolf mother.

"All the better to smell you with," replied his wolf mother.

One time they all discovered a giant Puma (cougar) standing over a freshly killed deer. There was blood everywhere in the snow.

The wolf mother growled hungrily so all the now bigger wolf pups growled to be like her and they were just as hungry. After a few more bites the Puma decided to abandon her deer meat as there were just too many wolves to tangle with. So the wolves moved in to share what was left of the dead deer, letting Mother Wolf have the first bite of many. Even the bones were eaten. Much, munch, munch.

Sometimes the hungry wolves even ate insects by licking them up with their tongues. Slurp, slurp, slurp.

The very next winter a snowboarder fell out of the

sky it seemed and landed eye to eye with Ronaldinho. Both were surprised!. After exchanging glances the snowboarder whizzed off down the mountainside.

There was a moon which seemed to talk and make faces through the clouds so every wolf and dog as well howled at it for its reply. There were comets and countless stars in the cold and freezing coyote nights. Then one day Ronaldinho's wolf mother lay down and was motionless with her eyes still open and her tongue stuck way out of her mouth. She did no longer breath and her eyes then glued shut and her body grew cold as the snow and rocks. She died.

All of her wolf children howled all night long to the angry moon which now shed some rainfall tears. One by one Ronaldinho's wolf brothers and sisters wandered off in different directions to different adventures hunting in Villa Angostura, El Bolson, Maiten and valley of the Black Glacier of Cerro Tronador.

So Ronaldinho was all alone now, he had never felt this lonely. So he began to search for a mate, a dog who might remind him of his mother Wolf or even his birth mother dog. There were some dogs at the base of Catedral Ski Mountain, even some Huskies with yellow and or blue eyes which are like wolf eyes. One of them had eyes like his wolf mother.

The two of them began to play at first in a game of I can catch you but can you catch me? This was very amusing to them and even spectators watching from a distance, very competitive also. Ronaldinho had to demonstrate that he was healthy and quick, fast and strong: that he would be a good father soon to her newborn puppies.

He was indeed. So they fell in love, Ronaldinho and the Husky sled dog and they ran away together up the slopes of Cerro Catedral into the snows of Pillin and Vuriloche. There she found a den for her puppies that were soon born and healthy.

But one day a Puma came and killed her and ate all the puppies while Ronaldinho was off hunting for Condor eggs, trout and deer carcasses. Then he returned home to her den and there was blood everywhere and his beloved was dead just like his wolf mother.

So Ronaldinho went down to the base of Catedral because he was starving and heartbroken. He had lost his entire family. Then a lady named Lynn came out of the building Salon de Te and brought him some leftover pizza the rich Portenos had left on the table uneaten to show off their great wealth. Then Lynn's father Ramon saw Ronaldinho from inside the steamy warm windows and brought him some bones and leftover meat.

Now Ronaldinho had a new home and people to love him even though he barely knew what love was he sensed it was very good indeed not like Pumas. He slept peacefully by the door but inside while skiers came and went, some asking questions about the dog that acts more like a wolf in the doorway.

"We named him Ronaldinho!" proclaimed Lynne and Ramon when asked. Ronaldinho was very fortunate to have a home as there are so many homeless dogs everywhere in Latin America. They live near restaurants and near bus stations and in the streets near markets and trash thrown into the street usually in plastic bags which they rip apart with their teeth to find tasty morsels. Very sad this is indeed because all that plastic blows in the wind to rivers to the ocean which kills fish and seabirds.

Then one day a foreigner tourist came to Salon de Te and his name was Ronaldinho. He was very rich and famous from Brazil where he played soccer. in the World Cup. He signed many autographs and starred in a movie. He asked Lynn what is the name of the dog in the doorway that looks more like a wolf and ignores everyone.

"O that is Ronaldinho named after you!" replied Lynn with Ramon's approval, "But he has had a very hard life in the mountains as he was mostly wild but now has chosen to come live with us!"

The movie star athlete wanted to pet the dog but Ronaldinho just growled at him.

"He doesn't like strangers," Ramon explained," Some people wanted to buy him because he's part wolf and they wanted to pay thousands of pesos but he's not for sale as he belongs to himself. He's his own dog and doesn't need a master. He's an Alpha wolf dog!" Lynee explained

"Oh that figures," said a passerby snowboarder who owned a wolf in another village.

Then one day the snowboarder who had almost crashed into Ronaldinho in Vuriloche on the slopes of Pillin came by to visit Lynn and asked,

"Where is that dog by the doorway, the one you call Ronaldinho?"

"Oh I am most sorry," said Ramon adding, "He

died last summer, a blue pickup truck ran him over on the road above here to the Tramway base. His face was smashed and he was just left to die there by that heartless drunk borracho. I found him and buried him by the big rock on a quiet path nearby I can show you"

"Oh how sad said the snowboarder. A year later the snowboarder married Lynn and Ramon retired from the restaurant to live on a meager pension and go fishing in a river of tears.

They didn't have any children right away, Lynn and her snowboarder husband. Maybe they were always snowboarding and too tired to hold hands and or kiss. So they decided to go to the pet store and adopt a puppy which had very big ears like Ronaldinho.

"What will you name this lucky puppy?" asked the silly lady at the pet store as she was so excited it would have a home.

"Ronaldinho!" exclaimed Lynn.

"Ronaldinho!" said the snowboarder at the very same moment.

The moon shone through the very fast moving windswept clouds of Alta Patagonia and seemed to be whispering to the little dog whose eyes were wild with excitement and he began to bark at it as it rose above the gargantuan Andes Mountains. They all lived happily ever after.

completed as the omnibus stopped in El Bolson by the writer and storyteller Duncan T Cullman copyright 2015

Party Central Brasil

The girl at the beach spoke broken English even though her girlfriends did not. She told me their boyfriends were coming to Ipanema after dark with knives and if they found me there with them I would be cut up into small pieces,

"They are trying to kill you," She added about my own parents.

"Yes, my stepmother doesn't like me" I agreed.

Then she suggested that I go into town where there are all night parties and just crash them for free drinks. The scenario was not good but free drinks were enticing to me as at age fifteen I was already a minor alcoholic. These girls were way too advanced for me though maybe just my own age they had been living there on this Ipanema like wild animals for several years as they ducked out of sight when police came looking for them. I didn't do drugs so I didn't realize they were "Mules" or drug traffickers for bigger dealers.

The sun was going down over the Sugarloaf and its large statue of Jesus Savior and cable car. The night life was about to declare itself in well lit mansions just a few blocks away. This young man of fifteen was eager and willing to take the hint these local young ladies were suggesting even though the alternative would be to lock myself in my little room with no television and nothing to do all night but wait until their big black boyfriends carded my lock.

"They will pick your lock and kill you" said my confidant and kissed me on the cheek.

"We tell you this for your own safety because you are a nice boy, we don't want to see you die so young and pretty"

I caught their drift and realized that even though there would be police patrols after dark that even police grow tired, eat doughnuts and drink coffee somewhere and tell jokes. I would get a stiletto and be bleeding. I left for the better lit streets of suburban CopaCabana and Rio. I met some young Brazilians my own age, one of whom spoke English. He said he was going to one of these parties for me to go with them to get invited in.

After a few drinks I was led to a room because I was not an invited guest. Were they going to call the police? No. The owner of the house came into the room to ask me,

"Where are your parents?"

"They are having dinner with the President of your country I think." was my reply.

"And they did not invite you?" was their reply. They looked at each other.

"Why are you wandering around in the streets, you are not old enough to be unchaperoned. Someone could put a pill in your drink. Are you aware or not?"

Again they looked at each other.

"Should we call the President?" One of them said.

"I will decide.," said the boss.

Then they said for me to stay there and sleep on the bed where I would be safe because they were leaving. I did sleep an hour but then I heard somebody screaming in the next room so I left the mansion entirely and went down the street where someone from my earlier companions said,

"There is the young American, invite him in!" So I was at another party until daylight. The sun was coming up over the ocean and seagulls were now screeching overhead announcing the new day.

"Come with us we'll get you some coffee" they invited me for a hot drink to warm me up. At the first opportunity I ran away as maybe they were planning to kidnap me. I was afraid. The sun was up on the beach when I finally returned to my room after ten oclock. My parents were there with two policemen.

"Where have you been, we'll miss the plane, dammit" said my step-mother."

"We can book another flight. Give me the telephone" said my father and he called the airport

Pulque and Picaniyeu

I agreed with my compadre Janko the Polish twenty four year old from Bariloche to accompany him to San Martin de los Andes, a six hour drive north from Bariloche. We had both been there before and now he convinced me that the place had changed for the better.

"One minor detail" he insisted, "You will have to ride in the trunk of my car past Pilcaniyeu as they don't let any Gringos near that place. It's top secret"

"Okay," I relented and three hours into our drive I jumped into the trunk of his car trustingly. I could hear him talking with the military guard at the roadblock. Argentina under Juan Peron had many such roadblocks and three times that many military police guarding them.

If you never lived or visited a fatchist country like Spain under Franco you cannot understand the subtle terror. The police in those countries have the right to shoot you on the spot with no questions asked. Everyone is very serious and quietly polite like in Nazi Germany.

The car started up again and after thirty minutes Janko stopped and let me out of the trunk. I think his family had been given instructions by the top Pole in Bariloche to get me out of town for a few weeks while some high ranking ex-Nazi officers would be visiting

Bariloche for some local ski competitions to which I was never invited or elligible. It was a very closed society that Bariloche opened only to families of ex-patriots of the Axis Powers who had fled there after World War II. Of course the Germans still considered themselves the master race and were mostly friendly only to others who believed them to be. Even the streetcars and buses had the horns that blasted noises like those in downtown Berlin, Germany.

"Dee doh, Dee doh!"

We arrived in San Martin and I was invited to the house of the very richest fellow in his magnificent hacienda more lavish then even the mansions of South Hampton on Long Island or at least equal in splendor but more like Montana log cabins or maybe Californian Sequoia tree cedar and redwood with numerous stocked ponds of Salmon more plentiful than Alaska.

Unfortunately I insulted my host who was expecting praise and thankfulness so I was ushered to the door after an elaborate ordoeuvre of salmon eggs, cheese and crackers. I displayed the intelligence of a ski racer which in most cases is an IQ of not above 115.

My host wanted to know what I had thought of Pilcaniyeu as I had not been in the car but must have passed by on foot taking surveillance photos for my government.

"I am sure my government has plenty of photos from its numerous satellites so why would I even bother with such a childish prank?"

"Yes but you needed to get into the hangar to see the "Pulque"! "he insisted.

"You mean to tell me that Argentina is still pursuing plans to construct a long range bomber capable of dropping a nuclear device on who? Brittain perhaps over those stupid little islands of yours, the Malvinas (Falklands)?

Why had Janko brought me here to this fellow unless perhaps they imagined in Bariloche that I was a trained spy. I definitely didn't consider myself as such. I was more a bard, a singing poet and mad skier. Now here were these people who imagined they were being spied upon probably because of this nuclear "Accelerator" Argentina had now built at Pilcaniyeu. It was by measurements fifty yards too short to refine weapons grade plutonium. Of course a ski racer like me was nor supposed to have any knowledge of physics other than loss of altitude increases velocity.

Janko and I were sitting at the bar of some far less desirable downtown Asado when thirty soldiers burst in and throwing chairs at us arrested both of us in handcuffs in less than three minutes. We were escorted to the local jail which had bars but no windows and thus no heat. It began snowing for three weeks. We were in separate cells and being interrogated daily. They had taken even our jackets but did bring us a slab of fat in warm water called a stew as there was even a solitary potato.

The camp commander spoke very broken English and trusted me with the axe to split all his firewood which I did until there was nothing left to split. It had been warmer near the fire inside the Comandante Headquarters but I was returned each evening to my

steel bunk which had no blanket to shiver through each night. Obviously I had said the wrong things to that spoiled brat who seemingly owned the entire village. They were planning to build this place San Martin into a major Argentine winter resort maybe after the nuclear war with Britain over the Falklands.

It doesn't seem logical to me to bomb London as it's all those Brits who frequently ski Switzerland who have created the big hotel industry there. After this nuclear war over the Falklands the tourists would be arriving here from a victorious Fourth Reich which is to appear out of thin air once the Pulque bomber version is perfected and those Brits and Gringos are on the defensive. Argentina with its thirty million people would somehow overpower Brazil and its one hundred fifty million of mostly slaves imported from Africa. Brazil had brought three times as many slaves over as the American Colonies had.

Finally they brought another prisoner into my cell but just for a gay. He was planted there to dig information from me so I told him about ski racing in the Alps and Chile until his ears could stand no more.

Then I was alone again. There was no more wood to split. I was then interviewed by a lawyer sent from Janko who had been released after torture revealed he knew even less than I about the Pulque bomber version or the nuclear reactor in Pilcaniyeu. A lawyer bailed me out but we skipped bail and drove straight back to Bariloche where I would ski one last week before my plane would leave for New York. Otto Skorzeny questioned me on

the ski slope and was puzzled to learn I had no idea who he was other than what he had told me,

"I was a machine gunner at Stalingrad but I ran out of bullets so I had to stab them all with my bayonet!" he had informed me of his WWII misadventures in the Wehrmacht.

Then shortly before I was to leave for town and my flight next morning Mengele had walked through the kitchen door in an apron with his medicine bag that included two duelling pistols which were rigged to fire backwards. I wanted to ask him about Nona Okun, the Whire Russian ten year old he sterilized but thought better than to provoke him. He had flu shots probably laced with gasoline, his favorite. So I was polite and told him I was a historian not a spy. He must have believed me because he knew and trusted the blond man, my father perhaps Hans Ulrich Rudel, Stuka pilot decorated by the Fuhrer himself in his bunker beneath Berlin.

When Liz came to shoot me

Liz and Dennis were a very fine young couple. I never should have interfered but I like beer still for probably well over twenty five years. I had been drinking it after work, I didn't work for myself, mostly for Peter Thurston the roofer, Jim Drew the foundation guy or at Ned Mulford's ski shop. All of these jobs in Telluride paid five dollars an hour, Jim a little more until he figured to cut our pay and we refused and were laid off. At least when I was young (under 45 yrs old) there were always more back breaking jobs or ski repair which included mostly smelling burning plastic. I thought I could work forever not realizing the Rocky Mountain minerals in the drinking water contained Lead Carbonate and other poisons that were a ticking time bomb.

Liz and Dennis dated since high school in Colorado Springs so they were already married but didn't know it. I was talking with her at the Floradora bar owned by Charlie Kane and Forie but managed by Howie Stern from Brooklyn with his wife Lois who let Howie do all the talking. He was an excellent baseball player like Yogi Berra but became a bartender manager not a New York Yankee. Liz worked there because she was gorgeous like all Howie's bar maids but it was her night off and she was sipping a Margarita and I began talking to her as she had sat beside me. She was of English extraction and I didn't realize she was part Italian until I did her tree on Ancestry.com decades later. Well those Italians have ample hips and chests. I began to wish I had a girl like her as my wife had run off to Santa Fe with her mother and my child.

I was camping out in an abandoned house for a few weeks at the time with no money for rent and working on my first novella, The Waitress, compiling its chapters and of course poems all written to Liz because she was an inspiration. So I hung my poems one day on her clothesline which was far too aggressive I admit.

Of course I got her attention. She was fuming mad down there in the street with her Italian girlfriend Kathy Tasconi but I was busy on the roof high above working for Peter Thurston, possibly the only nice guy in all of Telluride (there weren't very many as money had come to town_.

"You definitely got her attention!" observed Peter adding, "Maybe you should go down and talk to her?"

She was fuming mad and a woman and I had dealt with those for most of my life as I didn't have money, an ingredient that turns a woman's itr into ardour. Of course I was thinking of marrying her as mine had run off.

"Wrong again!" is what they say in these modern times.

Sure enough Liz came looking for me with a gun she must have borrowed from the Elks Club, "Best people on earth with guns also"

So I was sleeping with my dog Helga as my other

dog Spokey had died and we were at Sally Sarnoff's trailer in the trailer park which is no longer there under the avalanche cliffs near the abandoned mine at the east edge of town.

"I'm going to shoot him" I could hear Liz say to Dennis who had accompanied her but was trying to talk her out of it. Sally Sarnoff was not home and all her lights were off and the trailer dark as was the entire neighborhood at one o'clock in the morning.

"You don't want to involve other people" coached Dennis, her beloved beau who would within a year marry her officially.

My dog Helga let out a muffled bark from the woodshed where Sally said I might camp if she was not home.

"I know he's in there!" said Liz adding, "Come out and face justice!"

I think she pulled back the hammer. I decided to play dead possum and definitely I was not going to deal with any woman with a loaded gun. I had met them before and they when drunk are especially like wild animals.

Dennis finally talked her out of her irrational behavior and they left probably because Liz was passing out drunk. Usually I played with them in town co-ed soccer on opposing teams as mine was mostly Latinos including Julia Clemente Tallachea, the stone mason from near Bariloche, Argentina. He was an understudy of Pablito and Gran Pablo, Rossenkjer and Skorzeny as he had been on the Argentinme Olympic Ski Team that came to Squaw Valley, California 1964. Julian rore up his return ticket or sold it more likely to some Mexican for $100. We had John Palmer from Darien the striker and Leo MacNamara at fullback with me.

At any rate poor Liz had health problems, breast cancer and reductions a few years later. We were never on speaking terms as I had thyroid failure and went off the deep end in loneliness and drowning myself in beer and self-pity. She was a wonderful skier I enjoyed seeing her ski beneath lift 8 like a lioness. She was a shortstop at softball too though her soccer lacked sufficient speed. She developed multiple sclerosis or muscular dystrophy and died in Ridgeway. I never got to speak with her again but she was a schoolteacher for many years and well loved by her young students. Now she is a Telluride legend so are we all.

Pulque and Picaniyeu

I agreed with my compadre Janko the Polish twenty four year old from Bariloche to accompany him to San Martin de los Andes, a six hour drive north from Bariloche. We had both been there before and now he convinced me that the place had changed for the better.

"One minor detail" he insisted, "You will have to ride in the trunk of my car past Pilcaniyeu as they don't let any Gringos near that place. It's top secret"

"Okay," I relented and three hours into our drive I jumped into the trunk of his car trustingly. I could hear him talking with the military guard at the roadblock. Argentina under Juan Peron had many such roadblocks and three times that many military police guarding them.

If you never lived or visited a fatchist country like Spain under Franco you cannot understand the subtle terror. The police in those countries have the right to shoot you on the spot with no questions asked. Everyone is very serious and quietly polite like in Nazi Germany.

The car started up again and after thirty minutes Janko stopped and let me out of the trunk. I think his family had been given instructions by the top Pole in Bariloche to get me out of town for a few weeks while some high ranking ex-Nazi officers would be visiting

Bariloche for some local ski competitions to which I was never invited or elligible. It was a very closed society that Bariloche opened only to families of ex-patriots of the Axis Powers who had fled there after World War II. Of course the Germans still considered themselves the master race and were mostly friendly only to others who believed them to be. Even the streetcars and buses had the horns that blasted noises like those in downtown Berlin, Germany.

"Dee doh, Dee doh!"

We arrived in San Martin and I was invited to the house of the very richest fellow in his magnificent hacienda more lavish then even the mansions of South Hampton on Long Island or at least equal in splendor but more like Montana log cabins or maybe Californian Sequoia tree cedar and redwood with numerous stocked ponds of Salmon more plentiful than Alaska.

Unfortunately I insulted my host who was expecting praise and thankfulness so I was ushered to the door after an elaborate ordoeuvre of salmon eggs, cheese and crackers. I displayed the intelligence of a ski racer which in most cases is an IQ of not above 115.

My host wanted to know what I had thought of Pilcaniyeu as I had not been in the car but must have passed by on foot taking surveillance photos for my government.

"I am sure my government has plenty of photos from its numerous satellites so why would I even bother with such a childish prank?"

"Yes but you needed to get into the hangar to see the "Pulque"! "he insisted.

"You mean to tell me that Argentina is still pursuing plans to construct a long range bomber capable of dropping a nuclear device on who? Brittain perhaps over those stupid little islands of yours, the Malvinas (Falklands)?

Why had Janko brought me here to this fellow unless perhaps they imagined in Bariloche that I was a trained spy. I definitely didn't consider myself as such. I was more a bard, a singing poet and mad skier. Now here were these people who imagined they were being spied upon probably because of this nuclear "Accelerator" Argentina had now built at Pilcaniyeu. It was by measurements fifty yards too short to refine weapons grade plutonium. Of course a ski racer like me was nor supposed to have any knowledge of physics other than loss of altitude increases velocity.

Janko and I were sitting at the bar of some far less desirable downtown Asado when thirty soldiers burst in and throwing chairs at us arrested both of us in handcuffs in less than three minutes. We were escorted to the local jail which had bars but no windows and thus no heat. It began snowing for three weeks. We were in separate cells and being interrogated daily. They had taken even our jackets but did bring us a slab of fat in warm water called a stew as there was even a solitary potato.

The camp commander spoke very broken English and trusted me with the axe to split all his firewood which I did until there was nothing left to split. It had been warmer near the fire inside the Comandante Headquarters but I was returned each evening to my

steel bunk which had no blanket to shiver through each night. Obviously I had said the wrong things to that spoiled brat who seemingly owned the entire village. They were planning to build this place San Martin into a major Argentine winter resort maybe after the nuclear war with Britain over the Falklands.

It doesn't seem logical to me to bomb London as it's all those Brits who frequently ski Switzerland who have created the big hotel industry there. After this nuclear war over the Falklands the tourists would be arriving here from a victorious Fourth Reich which is to appear out of thin air once the Pulque bomber version is perfected and those Brits and Gringos are on the defensive. Argentina with its thirty million people would somehow overpower Brazil and its one hundred fifty million of mostly slaves imported from Africa. Brazil had brought three times as many slaves over as the American Colonies had.

Finally they brought another prisoner into my cell but just for a gay. He was planted there to dig information from me so I told him about ski racing in the Alps and Chile until his ears could stand no more.

Then I was alone again. There was no more wood to split. I was then interviewed by a lawyer sent from Janko who had been released after torture revealed he knew even less than I about the Pulque bomber version or the nuclear reactor in Pilcaniyeu. A lawyer bailed me out but we skipped bail and drove straight back to Bariloche where I would ski one last week before my plane would leave for New York. Otto Skorzeny questioned me on

the ski slope and was puzzled to learn I had no idea who he was other than what he had told me,

"I was a machine gunner at Stalingrad but I ran out of bullets so I had to stab them all with my bayonet!" he had informed me of his WWII misadventures in the Wehrmacht.

Then shortly before I was to leave for town and my flight next morning Mengele had walked through the kitchen door in an apron with his medicine bag that included two duelling pistols which were rigged to fire backwards. I wanted to ask him about Nona Okun, the Whire Russian ten year old he sterilized but thought better than to provoke him. He had flu shots probably laced with gasoline, his favorite. So I was polite and told him I was a historian not a spy. He must have believed me because he knew and trusted the blond man, my father perhaps Hans Ulrich Rudel, Stuka pilot decorated by the Fuhrer himself in his bunker beneath Berlin

Be A Soldier

I want you to be a soldier because this is a war on the Sars2 Virus that has invaded us. All these teachers, event organizers and sports personnel plus athletes: they are all taking the Covid Test at the Hospital Drive Thru sites weekly.

Do your part to reduce transmission. wash your hands and use hand sanitizer. wear your masks in public and large gatherings.

We can win this war if everybody joins our winning team. Get on board. Be a soldier. Be a team player and join our triumphant team. We want you on board our flag ship. we are all in this together.

Every week FrankTansey and the Vertical Challenge crew get tested before going to each and every Chevy sponsored event in any of nine different states. to bring you all the excitement of skiing and snowboarding mostly in the northeastern USA.

Yet in Europe it is no different for the FIS which sponsors the World Cups of skiing and snowboarding. All the athletes line up like soldiers and get tested before traveling to the next state. So there is no excuse for you to not be brave if we are all going to win this war against the virus and be healthy. We will all need to be vaccinated and stay home if sick.

I know you are brave because your parents were brave before you or they never would have been parents at all. Bravery and courage is inherent in all of us. We practice it daily on ski slopes and on mountaintops and on sports fields.

You can do this. You can join our army. You too can be a brave soldier and help win this fight for the survival of humanity.

I am thanking you for being brave. I am thanking you for being an athlete. I am thanking you for being on a winning team. Now go and have fun.

Have fun being brave and courageous. No one on this team is a wimp and no one on this team is a loser. You were born to win and be brave

We have a war to win

We have a war to win against this Sars2 virus

We have a Crusade to fight but dropping bombs and shooting bullets

At people who don't believe as we do will never suffice in bringing peace

Our God has many faces and we humans cannot see them all or we would go mad

Since our finite limited brains are not large enough with only a few million cells

In this universe of zillions of billions we are small yet not insignificant

We stand guard yes we are vigilant like the Guards of London who guard the Queen

We will fight only if we must and this Sars2 virus requires that we fight together

We have a war to win so wear your mask when not socially distancing

More of Jimmy On The Mountain

"Any day you can wake up in America and make a cup of coffee, even if you have no money at all, is a very good day indeed!" That is what Jimmy Thompson always said with a wide grin. Sometimes he would roll a joint and we would smoke one or two puffs of that stuff too then he would extinguish it and save what was left for just before he went to sleep.

He did have nightmares too and would wake up screaming thinking he was back there in "Nam", Vietnam in that battle that almost ended his life. A great big guy, his friend, took a bullet or two and fell on top of him dead. It saved his life at least for that very moment when the battle broke out. The 101rst had walked into a horseshoe shaped ambush with the NVR, North Vietnsmese regulars coming out of holes in the ground to catch the Americans in a deadly crossfire. Somehow, perhaps when darkness ensued, Jimmy managed to crawl under a tree which had been hit by a mortar so of course there was no tree left but a big dislodged root system with a hole under it. He continued to play dead. Only one other American was still alive in his vicinity and they could hear the NVR doing a body count of the Americans shooting anyone who was still alive. First light ensued and those NVR's in their pajamas were getting really close so they had to start shooting their very last magazines.

Luckily at that moment U.S. Navy Warthogs swooped down a dropped napalm narrowly missing them. There were the screams of those being roasted in burning plastic and the NVR that were still alive ran away.

Jimmy was Medevaced, evacuated by helicopter as his wounds were severe. He woke up in a Hospital Ship and then was flown back to the United States where he gave some lectures to green recruits about to be shipped out over there to "Nam". At least he now had hot coffee. After two months of this despite being constantly recruited to re-up which is re-enlist he fought off the temptation which for him was not so tempting at all. He had almost been killed and everyone in his platoon of over one hundred had been killed except for seven of them. He felt very good to be alive. He was relishing every good cup of hot coffee even if there was no cream or sugar. He was discharged and returned to his mother Rita's house in North Conway, New Hampshire. You can get there by bus from Boston in about five hours back then. Coming back to placid little New Hampshire was like returning to Fairy Land or Walt Disney with Mickey Mouse. People he met in the streets were mostly war protestors and very few thanked him for his service. These people whether they were for or against the war had almost no concept of total war other than Hogan's Heroes or Gomer Pyle. There were still some documentaries of Iwo Jima from WWII with the Marines using flamethrowers scalding everyone but until you can smell burning flesh and possibly your own you don't have any idea that you are totally expendable. The U.S. Military Industrial Complex WANTS YOU for cannon fodder.

So Jimmy and his young wife Cindy and their daughter Valerie headed for Taos, New Mexico to go live with the Indians. Many of those Indians had served in various wars as it was their opportunity to get a job and see the world plus receive the G.I. Bill and a few even went to college where they studied mostly agriculture or forestry. A few became lawyers and politicians. All the money in New Mexico is the Bank of Texas which managed to buy most of the farms in Eastern New Mexico leaving just the badlands and some hills in Western New Mexico to the Spanish and or Indians who inter marry, it is true. All the pure Indians, Navahos, Commanche and Apaches had mostly died of smallpox.

Jimmy liked it there in New Mexico living among some hippie communes until war broke out with some local badass Spanish who began shooting at them killing a few. The Sihks then bought a machine gun and fired back at the native Mexican Spanish-Indian mix badasses. Cindy had not been to war and was uneasy and left for Tamworth, New Hampshire to be with her mother. Me and Jimmy who I had originally met at Joe Jones ski shop in North Conway where he was a salesman, we hitchhiked to Pilar to play cards because we had no money at all and Jimmy thought he could win a few dollars if our hosts got very drunk late into the night. Jimmy won forty dollars and we were camping out with a guest host when our gracious hosts began taking pot shots at us at six o'clock in the morning. Bang. Bang. Bang.

"That means we are supposed to leave!" said Jimmy with a wide smile again adding,

"No time for coffee here this morning, we'll hitch to Taos and buy some on the Plaza. We had some money and we'd get some "Huevos Rancheros "with flour tortillas and Chili Verde(green sauce).

Jimmy told me he had once been camping in the mountains here with Charles Manson who had a gang. Some young little hippies overdosed possibly on heroin or cocaine. Rather than call the police the Manson gang just threw the dead bodies on the bonfire. That took care of that. Then the Mansons moved to Nevada and California to eventually kill a bunch of movie stars including Sharon Tate at her pool in Beverly Hills. What was left out of that story was that Richard Nixon had authorized with covert money the manufacture of "Jacob's Ladder" a type of LSD for use by the American military to use in battle and totally become psychotic and enjoy killing with no remorse whatsoever. There were laboratories funded by our own government all over the United States of America giving this stuff away at discount prices to any young or old hippy wanting to be a guinea pig for experimentation.

Jimmy then brought his Ecuadorian girlfriend to Silverton, Colorado where I had bought a mining claim and had been host to a handful of college graduate hippies from Ohio who had now run off to new adventures, Shawn was her name as she had at least one gringo parent. She made chipettes which were between pancakes and tortillas but very delicious. Jimmy made his coffee while I attended the fire adding dry sticks or the stove adding chopped fallen branches. We had a view of twin peaks over thirteen thousand feet. We were in my cabins that were beyond rustic on a mining claim eleven miles from town all uphill to this cabin site at eleven thousand nine hundred forty feet on the side of Bonita Peak.

I am not sure why we ever left but Shawn probably wanted to take a bath in town. We ran for water up there to nearby streams but had no running water to speak of.

Jimmy went to Washington, D.C. to teach many others the great lessons he had learned as I was not the best of students. He died there in 2010 among other Vietnam War Veterans and a whole flock of very devoted friends I am sure.

The warty hog
(Warthog and tank destroyer)

I applied for and received my new building permit from the town of Pagosa Springs, Colorado. I had bought a new patented mining claim high in a mountain valley above there. My friend Ben from Craig, Colorado would frame it for me as I was more the impatient wood butcher. His wife and children arrived by car and they all splashed naked like the hippies they had learned to be in Telluride at the Summer Jazz Festival there or elsewhere. His wife Kathleen was descended from Naples, Italy where the French Royal Family had fled when the Bourbon King, Louis the 14th had been beheaded in the French Revolution. Vive La France she was well endowed I could see from the distance. Her grandfather on one side she thought was a Turk but his name was really Turqu and he had been born in Tunisia, formerly Carthage the home of Hannibal who had ransacked Italy two thousand years ago.

I had sold my famous mining claim in Silverton, Colorado after a falling out with the other "Monks" I had recruited from the Grand Imperial Hotel Bar to live there. They were a collection of out-of-state tourists usually from colleges recently such as Ohio State. After I lost one two three girlfriends living there at 12,000 feet of altitude I decided that 10,000 feet of altitude was probably high enough and warmer as well for my new dwelling. The house was framed almost fully when I ran out of money to pay Ben so they all packed up and left leaving me there alone holding plywood in place while trying to nail it with the other one hand, not easy. One has to hold the nail on the side of the hammer then pluck it into position and hope it doesn't fall back out before the first hammer swing. Ben was such a genius anyway, so good to have had him as when I crashed my motorcycle in Ophir at 75 mph he had rebuilt it completely and sold it for me. My back was broken almost and no need of a motorcycle now anyway.

The backhoe driver showed up and dug the hole for the septic tank which would arrive the next day. I was in luck staring at a mansion someone had built across the valley. A friend of mine downtown had said for me to not go there as "They are watching that place!"

"Oh really?" I was still wondering who they might be when twenty cars pulled up to it just last evening. It was really a big family, obviously. What a place to build a ski house with only snowmobile access in winter or else by X-C skis.

There were a lot of scraps of wood I could now throw away plus this oversize tractor tire that was much too big to load on my car. Maybe I could just throw everything in that septic hole and burn it to avoid an expensive trip to the faraway town dump. Besides, who would see me up here in the middle of nowhere. Maybe some satellites or a distant hiker on a 13,800 ft peak in the distance. I had climbed on these ridges a few different evenings and seen what appear to be cell towers or reflection towers which seem to be a go between the mysterious mansion and Pikes Peak near Colorado Springs way off in the distance but still visible from the ridgetops above me.

So I light the fire early the next morning as the septic is not due until mid afternoon. A big plume of white smoke rises but turns black when the fire reaches the giant tire. It's really a hot flame now as that synthetic rubber burns really hot, maybe a temperature like a missile being launched by a bunker at Moscow or the Commies. Their satellites must be up there as well overhead somewhere beyond the blue sky.

Suddenly I hear this roar like a loud thunderstorm but there is no cloud in sight and no lightning but the echoes are off every mountainside and it is getting very loud indeed so I look up just in time to see a pilots eyeballs looking out of the cockpit of a tank destroying aircraft like a Navy Harrier but maybe it's an Air Force jet flying at over 400 mph he straightens out his wings as he had been flying sideways over me then with a tremendous roar the plane climbs straight up into the sky with a sonic boom deafening my ears.

"Maybe I better put out this fire very quickly?" I realize the truth of these few seconds being most revealing. I shovel dirt on the fire and the black smoke turns white again eventually as the big flames are snuffed out.

The very next day a Forest Ranger tells me he had seen the smoke and what exactly was I burning beside construction garbage? A few days later more than twenty gendarme of the state variety swing by and park their

ATV's and their fearless leader, a captain or lieutenant asks me politely about some bullshit story I made up about a Nazi pilot in Argentina. Could I please verify the story and describe exactly the car in full as I was full of shit.

"Well, it was I think a stainless steel 1953 Porsche 911 with the driver's side door welded shut and unusable because there was a lever on the driver's left side since he had only one leg. We had entered the car, him first, from the passenger's side only door. He promised to take me somewhere where the man in charge wanted to see my French Skis, Rossignol 210 cm I had purchased in Portillo from Jean Claude killy and Michelle Arpin but the bases were falling off as the glue had been inferior so that maybe is why they sold them to me for $120." I nailed the story exactly as it had happened in 1964 thirty years before.

Finally I told the twenty curious state employees that I would probably sell the property as I wasn't extraordinarily wealthy. A cocktail waitress named Tammy had expressed an interest in buying it after she gave me the sob story of her life which, unknown to me, was pure bullshit. Actually her family built all the private prisons in Colorado including the one that currently was holding the top living Al-Qaeda prisoner from Guantanamo, Cuba military detention center recently which was to be closed very soon altogether.

They seemed content in the fact that I would most probably be leaving their state soon and not be in their hair anymore. What were all these complaints about me and from where I will never know. Possibly it was my father's home office in New York trying to extract me from Colorado because I had visited my ex-wife with a machine gun muttering,

"They're after me still those motherfuckers!"

She must have told my father Louise, no doubt and he told the FBI?

I don't think there is any freedom in this country other than freedom to get a job or go straight to jail :the American Way!

I had inherited some money from my maternal grandmother and mother who passed in quick succession and I had thought I might reinvest some of it in Rocky Mountain high property where all the hippies like to get high. More than likely my ex-wife was having designs on my investments and wanted all my property. I would just have to leave this happy hippy state and travel east once again as my own father would continually beckon me back to Connecticut for a dinner with the "Family". Yes there were a lot of them, both rich and poor. My father's current wife's children were threatening to sue him and they lived up to their promises as soon as she died.

My step-mother had bought a ton of art in Indonesia with my own father's money but the written checks and bills of sale said, "Dorothy Coleman". She was indeed the wicked witch of the East from the Wizard of Oz and soon enough my own father's property would be denuded by these ravaging parasitic stepsons Freddie and Billie Benevolentson, one a principal of a school and the other a Hollywood film director.

I am thinking about all this while at Myrtle Beach

telling these stories to "My brother" Walter Godsmark whose dog has a big smile on his face like he has just eaten a big prime rib rare and his belly is wonderfully full. So is Walter's. They left the next morning for Atlanta, happy as clams indeed...

The Warty Hog(Warthog, harrier jet) all our condolences for your dog who has left his former life behind Sherlock Holmes to be a brand new dog Comstock Gunstock" Meat eater gargantuan

Pulque and Picaniyeu

I agreed with my compadre Janko the Polish twenty four year old from Bariloche to accompany him to San Martin de los Andes, a six hour drive north from Bariloche. We had both been there before and now he convinced me that the place had changed for the better.

"One minor detail" he insisted, "You will have to ride in the trunk of my car past Pilcaniyeu as they don't let any Gringos near that place. It's top secret"

"Okay," I relented and three hours into our drive I jumped into the trunk of his car trustingly. I could hear him talking with the military guard at the roadblock. Argentina under Juan Peron had many such roadblocks and three times that many military police guarding them.

If you never lived or visited a fatchist country like Spain under Franco you cannot understand the subtle terror. The police in those countries have the right to shoot you on the spot with no questions asked. Everyone is very serious and quietly polite like in Nazi Germany.

The car started up again and after thirty minutes Janko stopped and let me out of the trunk. I think his family had been given instructions by the top Pole in Bariloche to get me out of town for a few weeks while some high ranking ex-Nazi officers would be visiting

Bariloche for some local ski competitions to which I was never invited or elligible. It was a very closed society that Bariloche opened only to families of ex-patriots of the Axis Powers who had fled there after World War II. Of course the Germans still considered themselves the master race and were mostly friendly only to others who believed them to be. Even the streetcars and buses had the horns that blasted noises like those in downtown Berlin, Germany.

"Dee doh, Dee doh!"

We arrived in San Martin and I was invited to the house of the very richest fellow in his magnificent hacienda more lavish then even the mansions of South Hampton on Long Island or at least equal in splendor but more like Montana log cabins or maybe Californian Sequoia tree cedar and redwood with numerous stocked ponds of Salmon more plentiful than Alaska.

Unfortunately I insulted my host who was expecting praise and thankfulness. So I was ushered to the door after an elaborate ordoeuvre of salmon eggs, cheese and crackers. I displayed the intelligence of a ski racer which in most cases is an IQ of not above 115.

My host wanted to know what I had thought of Pilcaniyeu as I had not been in the car but must have passed by on foot taking surveillance photos for my government.

"I am sure my government has plenty of photos from its numerous satellites so why would I even bother with such a childish prank?"

"Yes but you needed to get into the hangar to see the "Pulque"! "he insisted.

"You mean to tell me that Argentina is still pursuing plans to construct a long range bomber capable of dropping a nuclear device on who? Brittain perhaps over those stupid little islands of yours, the Malvinas (Falklands)?

Why had Janko brought me here to this fellow unless perhaps they imagined in Bariloche that I was a trained spy. I definitely didn't consider myself as such. I was more a bard, a singing poet and mad skier. Now here were these people who imagined they were being spied upon probably because of this nuclear "Accelerator" Argentina had now built at Pilcaniyeu. It was by measurements fifty yards too short to refine weapons grade plutonium. Of course a ski racer like me was nor supposed to have any knowledge of physics other than loss of altitude increases velocity.

Janko and I were sitting at the bar of some far less desirable downtown Asado when thirty soldiers burst in and throwing chairs at us arrested both of us in handcuffs in less than three minutes. We were escorted to the local jail which had bars but no windows and thus no heat. It began snowing for three weeks. We were in separate cells and being interrogated daily. They had taken even our jackets but did bring us a slab of fat in warm water called a stew as there was even a solitary potato.

The camp commander spoke very broken English and trusted me with the axe to split all his firewood which I did until there was nothing left to split. It had been warmer near the fire inside the Comandante Headquarters but I was returned each evening to my

steel bunk which had no blanket to shiver through each night. Obviously I had said the wrong things to that spoiled brat who seemingly owned the entire village. They were planning to build this place San Martin into a major Argentine winter resort maybe after the nuclear war with Britain over the Falklands.

It doesn't seem logical to me to bomb London as it's all those Brits who frequently ski Switzerland who have created the big hotel industry there. After this nuclear war over the Falklands the tourists would be arriving here from a victorious Fourth Reich which is to appear out of thin air once the Pulque bomber version is perfected and those Brits and Gringos are on the defensive. Argentina with its thirty million people would somehow overpower Brazil and its one hundred fifty million of mostly slaves imported from Africa. Brazil had brought three times as many slaves over as the American Colonies had.

Finally they brought another prisoner into my cell but just for a gay. He was planted there to dig information from me so I told him about ski racing in the Alps and Chile until his ears could stand no more.

Then I was alone again. There was no more wood to split. I was then interviewed by a lawyer sent from Janko who had been released after torture revealed he knew even less than I about the Pulque bomber version or the nuclear reactor in Pilcaniyeu. A lawyer bailed me out but we skipped bail and drove straight back to Bariloche where I would ski one last week before my plane would leave for New York. Otto Skorzeny questioned me on

the ski slope and was puzzled to learn I had no idea who he was other than what he had told me,

"I was a machine gunner at Stalingrad but I ran out of bullets so I had to stab them all with my bayonet!" he had informed me of his WWII misadventures in the Wehrmacht.

Then shortly before I was to leave for town and my flight next morning Mengele had walked through the kitchen door in an apron with his medicine bag that included two duelling pistols which were rigged to fire backwards. I wanted to ask him about Nona Okun, the Whire Russian ten year old he sterilized but thought better than to provoke him. He had flu shots probably laced with gasoline, his favorite. So I was polite and told him I was a historian not a spy. He must have believed me because he knew and trusted the blond man, my father perhaps Hans Ulrich Rudel, Stuka pilot decorated by the Fuhrer himself in his bunker beneath Berlin

When Liz came to shoot me

Liz and Dennis were a very fine young couple. I never should have interfered but I like beer still for probably well over twenty five years. I had been drinking it after work, I didn't work for myself, mostly for Peter Thurston the roofer, Jim Drew the foundation guy or at Ned Mulford's ski shop. All of these jobs in Telluride paid five dollars an hour, Jim a little more until he figured to cut our pay and we refused and were laid off. At least when I was young (under 45 yrs old) there were always more back breaking jobs or ski repair which included mostly smelling burning plastic. I thought I could work forever not realizing the Rocky Mountain minerals in the drinking water contained Lead Carbonate and other poisons that were a ticking time bomb.

Liz and Dennis dated since high school in Colorado Springs so they were already married but didn't know it. I was talking with her at the Floradora bar owned by Charlie Kane and Forie but managed by Howie Stern from Brooklyn with his wife Lois who let Howie do all the talking. He was an excellent baseball player like Yogi Berra but became a bartender manager not a New York Yankee. Liz worked there because she was gorgeous like all Howie's bar maids but it was her night off and she was sipping a Margarita and I began talking to her as she had sat beside me. She was of English extraction and I didn't realize she was part Italian until I did her tree on Ancestry.com decades later. Well those Italians have ample hips and chests. I began to wish I had a girl like her as my wife had run off to Santa Fe with her mother and my child.

I was camping out in an abandoned house for a few weeks at the time with no money for rent and working on my first novella, The Waitress, compiling its chapters and of course poems all written to Liz because she was an inspiration. So I hung my poems one day on her clothesline which was far too aggressive I admit.

Of course I got her attention. She was fuming mad down there in the street with her Italian girlfriend Kathy Tasconi but I was busy on the roof high above working for Peter Thurston, possibly the only nice guy in all of Telluride (there weren't very many as money had come to town_.

"You definitely got her attention!" observed Peter adding, "Maybe you should go down and talk to her?"

She was fuming mad and a woman and I had dealt with those for most of my life as I didn't have money, an ingredient that turns a woman's itr into ardour. Of course I was thinking of marrying her as mine had run off.

"Wrong again!" is what they say in these modern times.

Sure enough Liz came looking for me with a gun she must have borrowed from the Elks Club, "Best people on earth with guns also"

So I was sleeping with my dog Helga as my other

dog Spokey had died and we were at Sally Sarnoff's trailer in the trailer park which is no longer there under the avalanche cliffs near the abandoned mine at the east edge of town.

"I'm going to shoot him" I could hear Liz say to Dennis who had accompanied her but was trying to talk her out of it. Sally Sarnoff was not home and all her lights were off and the trailer dark as was the entire neighborhood at one o'clock in the morning.

"You don't want to involve other people" coached Dennis, her beloved beau who would within a year marry her officially.

My dog Helga let out a muffled bark from the woodshed where Sally said I might camp if she was not home.

"I know he's in there!" said Liz adding, "Come out and face justice!"

I think she pulled back the hammer. I decided to play dead possum and definitely I was not going to deal with any woman with a loaded gun. I had met them before and they when drunk are especially like wild animals.

Dennis finally talked her out of her irrational behavior and they left probably because Liz was passing out drunk. Usually I played with them in town co-ed soccer on opposing teams as mine was mostly Latinos including Julia Clemente Tallachea, the stone mason from near Bariloche, Argentina. He was an understudy of Pablito and Gran Pablo, Rossenkjer and Skorzeny as he had been on the Argentinme Olympic Ski Team that came to Squaw Valley, California 1964. Julian rore up his return ticket or sold it more likely to some Mexican for $100. We had John Palmer from Darien the striker and Leo MacNamara at fullback with me.

At any rate poor Liz had health problems, breast cancer and reductions a few years later. We were never on speaking terms as I had thyroid failure and went off the deep end in loneliness and drowning myself in beer and self-pity. She was a wonderful skier I enjoyed seeing her ski beneath lift 8 like a lioness. She was a shortstop at softball too though her soccer lacked sufficient speed. She developed multiple sclerosis or muscular dystrophy and died in Ridgeway. I never got to speak with her again but she was a schoolteacher for many years and well loved by her young students. Now she is a Telluride legend so are we all.

Perfect Pet

Like good parents me and Mommy

Guided our entire family on the Ark

Through the floodwaters of this horrible pandemic

We stayed home a lot or went for tennis or walks in the woods

With our dogs and cat who are likewise brave

Full of courage we stood up against that tyrant who tried to steal our democracy

We huddled together on the couch and watched the news reports

Our capitol overrun by thugs and neo-nazis of the KKK

We posted our defiance and resistance on facebook and instagram

The world is watching us because it rests upon our shoulders

Like a large bag of dog food or a crate of catfood

Bring the kitty litter to where the Donald has let loose his ite

My small dog has a terminal illness called life I
don't think she will live to see spring and the earth's
rejuvenation

Sad it is to think our lovely child may not be with us
on the long summer day

When peace shall be restored after this long viral WAR

Maybe she will suddenly get better or maybe she will
be released from her pain and suffering

Her loving eyes tell me she gave us all she had in this
her total life to be our loving family

I found her homeless in the streets of Chile five thousand
miles away

I brought her home only with the help of endless friends
against the wishes of my father

What does he know of love the vast fortune he spent
on his loves

Though his were not dogs or cats so much

My ancestors were Powhattan chiefs of the Wolf Clan

So wolves are in my blood and are family my little dog
knows

She tells me with her eyes though one is clouding over
with disease

Her thoughts for my well being are obvious she loves
me as life itself

I cannot thank her enough nor any other for walking my path so long

Please my God be gentle and kind with her she is so wonderful

Raise her up into your bosom of love and let her fly with your seraphim to guard your throne

She will behold your brilliance that you are love itself

She will make a perfect pet and long for you forevermore

CPSIA information can be obtained
at www.ICGtesting.com
Printed in the USA
LVHW031707180522
719074LV00003B/274

9 781954 886513